— VICTORIOUS LIVIN

THE
ARMOR
OF LIGHT

The Secrets of God's Protection

MICHAEL CHRISTIAN

TWIN PILLARS
PRESS
PARADISE • CALIFORNIA

ISBN 978-0-9894610-0-9

Library of Congress Control Number: 2020907091

Pronouns in Scripture that refer to the Father, Son, or Holy Spirit are capitalized intentionally to honor Him.

Contact Michael Christian at MichaelChristian.us

Publisher: TwinPillarsPress.com

*To all who labor to hear
the whispers of the Spirit and
translate them into simple words*

Contents

Foreword

Mike Christian has served our church in ministry for the last twenty-five years as a teaching pastor and in many other ways. He is a good friend like few others and of great understanding in the Word of God. After an accident years ago, he spent much time copying out Scriptures. As a result, his knowledge of the Bible is profound. This book is more than mere information but contains keys to living a victorious and overcoming life. With great pleasure I recommend *The Armor of Light*. Your life will be changed forever.

—STEVE GRANDY
Senior Pastor
Jubilee on the Ridge Church
Paradise, California

Preface

Like so many, I grew up in spiritual darkness. My family went to a Christian church, but it was not a Bible-teaching church, so I received little light from God's Word to guide me. After I left home for a secular college, I adopted the philosophies of my peers, followed my desires, made lots of mistakes, and quickly found myself confused and oppressed. I knew the answer was spiritual, but my Sunday School Christianity didn't seem to have the answers.

Fortunately, someone shared the simple Gospel with me, and (after asking dozens of questions) I accepted Christ as my Savior and was born again. Then I began to read the Bible in earnest, and it made sense for the first time. Thus began my journey out of the cave of spiritual darkness.

The Lord once said, "My people are destroyed for lack of knowledge,"[1] and that certainly applied to me. The consequences of unenlightened decisions followed me for years, and ignorance kept me in the dark about God's love, power, and blessings. When I accepted Christ, despite my new desire to live in His light, the darkness did not release its grip immediately. I hungered for a book like this one that would get me up to speed quickly.

As a new Christian, I pleaded with the Lord to make me wiser than the unseen enemies attacking my mind.[2] I felt condemned for a past I

---

[1] Hosea 4:6
[2] Psalm 119:97–104

could not change and for which I barely felt forgiven. In pursuit of answers and inner peace, I did one thing right—I meditated in the Bible day and night.

You can find more on my story and how God used a nearly fatal accident on an oil rig to radically change my lifestyle at…

https://michaelchristian.us/accident

As I read and hand copied God's Word consistently for many years, the Lord gradually freed me from the grip of bad attitudes, low self-esteem, and self-undermining ways of thought. Truly I was transformed by the renewing of my mind. I discovered who I was in Christ and set priorities more like His.[3] Meditating in the Bible's wisdom drew me closer to an awesome God, but I still had to fight my way upstream against the cultural currents, like a salmon hurtling rapids, to step into my destiny as a child of God.

I pray that you won't be the victim of darkness, ignorance, your past life, and invisible forces you cannot see any longer—*you can live victoriously in the light of a bright, new day in Christ!*

—MICHAEL CHRISTIAN

---

[3]   John 8:31–32, Philippians 2:5, Romans 12:2

Introduction

You can't fight a war with your eyes closed. Putting on the armor of God is about opening your spiritual eyes and turning from darkness to light.[4] Jesus said, "I AM the light of the world. He who follows Me shall not walk in darkness but have the light of life."[5]

The apostle John described the glorious impact of the light of Christ, "And the light shines in the darkness, and the darkness did not comprehend it."[6] The darkness cannot understand, overpower, or extinguish the light that's in Jesus Christ. For this reason, when we fill ourselves with His light, we have victory over the darkness and everything in it. However, our eyes need to adjust to living in the light.

The parable of the cave

Two boys knew each other only by the sound of their voices. One lived in a cave, and the other under the sun. One day the boy in the cave invited the other to come play with him. As he walked out of the sunshine into the darkness, he exclaimed, "It's so dark in here, I can't see anything!" His new friend responded, "Just wait a few minutes, and your eyes will adjust to the dark."

They played a while, then the boy from the outside invited his friend to come see the sun and the blue sky. Once in the light, the boy

---

4   Acts 26:18
5   John 8:12, see also John 12:46
6   John 1:5

from the cave complained, "It's so bright out here. The light hurts my eyes, and I can't see anything!" His friend replied, "It will be okay. Just wait a few minutes, and your eyes will adjust to the light."

Once his eyes were accustomed to the sunshine, the boy could see for miles. "Wow! I didn't know there was so much out here. Just look at these colors! We don't see like this in the cave. In this light I can see forever."

When all we know is spiritual darkness and shades of gray, our mind adjusts to the darkness, and we think it's normal. But when we move into the light of Christ, it takes time for our mind to adapt. But when it does, we can see like we've never seen before—all the way to eternity!

My story

When I became a Christian, I thought I would never have another bad day. But I quickly found myself like those in the Parable of the Sower who received the good seed on stony ground. My new life sprang up with joy, but the heat of misunderstanding and trouble tried to wither me before I could become grounded and established. Plus, it was hard to grow roots in Christ through the stony places of brokenness, pain, and self-centeredness in my heart. I had to fight for my spiritual life, and I am thankful to those who stood by, prayed, and mentored me in those challenging early days. This was not an easy time.

As it slowly dawned on me that my Yes to Jesus had thrust me into a spiritual conflict, I became frustrated with the Lord. Why had He made things this way? Was I a sacrificial pawn in some cruel, cosmic chess match between God and the devil? Why was I being attacked for doing what was right for once? It made no sense. I found myself plunged into a struggle for which I had no training, no equipment, and little success. Higher education had failed to prepare me for spiritual realities.

Gradually, through the light of God's Word, I learned to identify my enemy, resist him, and stand my ground. The Lord set my feet on a solid rock and taught my heart to make war, not against people, but against the adversary of all that is good.

But more than that, as I relaxed and matured in Christ, I discovered I could thrive in the light by focusing on the Lord and His Word rather than worrying constantly about the dark side. While that realization did not stop the resistance completely, it allowed my spirit to flourish in a positive, peaceful framework without rejecting or ignoring the struggle. Paul said:

> If then you were raised with Christ, seek those things which are above, where Christ is, sitting at the right hand of God.
> —*Colossians 3:1*

As I've journeyed, I've learned some things that have set me free from inner turmoil, sin, discouragement, bad attitudes, low self-esteem, and ignorance of the ways of the Lord. Every chapter deals with a separate subject, but at the end of each one I relate a spiritual secret that will help you live in faith, victory, and peace.

Reborn as warriors

Although God is best described as a Father, He is also a warrior. As His children, we have been reborn in His image, and we are warriors. Because of Jesus, we have a full set of weapons to live victoriously—the blood of Jesus, the name of Jesus, and the Word of God. Plus, the Lord has given us His armor, the armor of light, to make us strong in battle.

> The night is far spent, the day is at hand. Therefore let us cast off the works of darkness, and let us put on *the armor of light.*
> —*Romans 13:12 (italics added)*

But our Father does something more: He fills us with Himself so we can experience His love. Our battle becomes His battle—the battle is the Lord's[7]—and He fights through us. When we feel overwhelmed, His Spirit rises within us to fight another day and win. The inner light of Christ gives victory over darkness in all its forms.

Overview of the book

This book offers you nineteen secrets of thriving in the light of Christ. It describes the victory of Jesus, our covenant with God, how to receive light from the Word, the mysteries of the spiritual realm, and what you should know about holy and unholy angels. It includes chapters on your right to use the name of Jesus, the necessity of prayer, the

---

[7]   2 Chronicles 20:15

blood of Jesus, the Holy Spirit, wisdom, controlling your tongue, how to tell if it's God or the devil, and many other helpful subjects.

The armor of light

The final chapter is devoted to putting on the armor of God as the armor of light. The frequently-discussed pieces of Roman armor are simply metaphors for the seven light-filled *revelations* from God's Word that make up the real armor. After you read this chapter, you'll better understand the process of defending yourself.

So, welcome to spiritual boot camp! With a little faith, effort, and practice, you'll learn to use the weapons of your warfare to protect yourself and your family and live an overcoming life.

A non-linear book

Each chapter is written to more or less stand on its own. Though the first six chapters are foundational, read the book in any order you wish. I've found that I grow the fastest when I pursue the subjects in which I'm most interested, and then double back on the others. You'll find nuggets of truth to help you in every chapter.

The Victorious Living Series

Originally, I wrote this book as one rather full volume. To make it easier to digest, I've split it into a three-part series called *Victorious Living.* Each volume builds on the one before it. *The Armor of Light* is Volume 1.

Volume 2 is entitled *Tearing Down Strongholds: How to Fight the Good Fight of Faith.* In it I identify life's most common battlegrounds—the mind, the flesh, personal relationships, and fighting the good fight of faith. It teaches you how to use the shield of faith to extinguish the flaming thought arrows the enemy shoots into your mind. If left to burn, these will build strongholds in your mind, will, and emotions that will hold you in bondage for years. You need strategies for tearing down these strongholds, overcoming your flesh, protecting your relationships, and keeping the Word of God between you and your problems. The book includes original illustrations, prayers, and a life secret at the end of each chapter.

Declarations of Truth: How to Pray God's Word with Authority is Volume 3. The perfect companion to Volumes 1 and 2, *Declarations of Truth* provides inspired prayers and Scripture-based affirmations to help you demolish personal strongholds in over fifty areas of life. Breakthrough comes as you wield the sword of the Spirit—the uttered Word of God. As you declare Scripture aloud, you create seismic shifts in your spiritual atmosphere.

Read with Bible in hand

Christians today are often not familiar with the Bible. To help you locate important verses, I have footnoted extensively. It's one thing for me to share a scriptural principle, but that thought takes on life-changing authority when you read it for yourself in your own Bible. You must know God's truth (and apply it) before it can set you free.

God-given freedom

God gave you a purpose, and it's something you are good at doing that helps other people. It satisfies you in a way nothing else will. He knows who He designed you to be, what fulfills you in the core of your being, and how to stir up the gifts He gave you. As you do your part to serve Him, He frees you to be who He called you to be. By putting on the armor of light and pursuing your God-given dreams, you will live in Jesus' joy and victory.

CHAPTER ONE

The Ultimate Showdown!

"Or how can one enter a strong man's house and plunder his goods,
unless he first binds the strong man? And then he will plunder his
house." —Matthew 12:29

In ancient wars, opposing armies sometimes sent their top warrior into the no man's land between the armies to fight a man-to-man, winner-take-all battle. This was the battle of champions. You may be familiar with young David, who represented the army of Israel against Goliath, the supersized Philistine warrior.[1] David prevailed in the name of the LORD and killed the giant with a sling and a stone.

A thousand years later another young man, a direct descendant of David named Jesus, stood up as *mankind's champion* against the leader of the demonic underworld. This was the greatest spiritual battle of all time as Jesus, the Spirit-filled Savior, confronted the devil and his fallen angels. Kingdom faced off against kingdom—the purity, integrity, and might of the heavenly Man against the evil trickery of hell itself. Jesus defeated the devil by His cross and resurrection and forever freed those who believe in Him from the enemy's domination.[2]

Jesus fought for mankind

When Jesus died on the cross, though, it looked as if heaven had lost and evil had won. Despair settled over Christ's disciples. Had they

---

[1]   1 Samuel 17
[2]   Colossians 1:13

believed for three years in vain? But when Jesus rose from the dead, He had defeated the devil in the bowels of hell, taken from him the keys of death and Hades,[3] and released from their cells the souls of the righteous dead. He then led them in a triumphant victory procession from the underworld into the third heaven itself, entering through the beautiful gates into the glorious City of the New Jerusalem. For the first time, the gates of the kingdom of heaven opened wide for men.

> *When you become a believer in Jesus, your name is written in the Lamb's Book of Life. As one of His registered representatives, you carry a divine power of attorney—the official right to use the name of Jesus.*

There's never been such a magnificent parade. It was more impressive than the victory celebration of any human conqueror because Jesus, as an army of One, paid the ultimate price, invaded, conquered, and plundered hell of the souls of the righteous.[4] I can imagine Abraham rejoicing to see Christ's day, David dancing before the Lord like he never had before, the prophets prophesying of the good things to come, and the people of God singing and shouting at the top of their voices. And Satan and his forces were powerless to stop Him!

What just happened? The ultimate battle for the souls of men had been fought and won by Jesus. By overcoming the devil, He restored what man lost: our *relationship* with God and our *authority* under God.

The name of Jesus is above every name

As earth's undisputed Champion and King, Jesus earned a name that is above every name. Paul described Jesus' victory like this:

> And being found in appearance as a man, He humbled Himself and became obedient to the point of death, even the death of the cross. Therefore God also has highly exalted Him and given Him the name

---

[3]   Revelation 1:18
[4]   2 Corinthians 2:14–16, Ephesians 4:8–10, Daniel 7:13–14

which is above every name, that at the name of Jesus every knee should bow, of those in heaven, and of those on earth, and of those under the earth, and that every tongue should confess that Jesus Christ is Lord, to the glory of God the Father.

—Philippians 2:8–11

God gave Jesus "the Name which is above every name, that at the name of Jesus every knee should bow…" No other religious leader laid down his life for mankind, defeated the devil, made atonement for sins, and opened the way for mankind to enter heaven. We cannot say such things about Abraham, Moses, Buddha, Mohammed, Confucius, Mary, or anyone other than Jesus.

When you struggle with fear, guilt, or doubt, remember the victory Jesus won for you and all mankind. When you need help with addiction, demons, sickness, poverty, trouble, or persecution, call on Him who has proven power over all evil. Jesus' name has authority reverberating through three realms—heaven, earth, and hell itself. To Him every knee must bow!

Everything in your life needs to be built on the victory of Jesus. He is that solid rock foundation that cannot be shaken or moved in the storms of life.

You have authority in the name of Jesus

Then the seventy returned with joy, saying, "Lord, even the demons are subject to us *in Your name.*" And He said to them, "I saw Satan fall like lightning from heaven. Behold, I give you the *authority* to trample on serpents and scorpions, and over all the power of the enemy, *and nothing shall by any means hurt you.* Nevertheless do not rejoice in this, that the spirits are subject to you, but rather rejoice because *your names are written in heaven.*"

—Luke 10:17–20 (italics added)

When you become a believer in Jesus, your name is recorded in the Lamb's Book of Life. As His registered representative, you carry a divine power of attorney—the official right to use the name of Jesus. As a believer, you possess authority from the third heaven to use in the second heaven and on earth. I'll explain the three heavens in Chapter Four.

All authority in heaven and earth belongs to Jesus. If He has *all* authority, then other forces and powers have *none.* Fortunately, He shares His authority with those who believe in Him.[5] Christ has transferred us out from under the devil's dominion into the kingdom of God, so we are no longer the devil's victims.

> He has delivered us from the power of darkness and conveyed us into the kingdom of the Son of His love.
>
> —*Colossians 1:13*

> *Father, thank You for a right relationship with You because of what Jesus did for me. I put my trust and faith in Him. Therefore, in Jesus' mighty and powerful name I command the forces of darkness, including _____ , to depart from me and my family. We are under God's protection. In Jesus' name, I pray. Amen.*

You are raised to God's right hand

Not only do you have the right to speak in Jesus' name, you have a new position in Him. When you accepted Jesus as Savior, you became one with Him. As believers, we are spiritually united with Jesus in His death, burial, *and resurrection.* When He was crucified, we were crucified with Him. When He was buried, we were buried with Him.[6] When He was raised, we were raised with Him to His place of authority at God's right hand, far above all "principalities and powers" (the demonic spiritual forces in the second heaven).

> ...and what is the exceeding greatness of His power toward us who believe, according to the working of His mighty power which He worked in Christ when He raised Him from the dead and seated Him at His right hand in the heavenly places, *far above all principality and power and might and dominion, and every name that is named, not only in this age but also in that which is to come.* And He put all things under

---

[5]   Matthew 28:18–20 If this is a new concept to you, I strongly suggest you read one or more of the excellent books that explain the authority that belongs to believers. This teaching is foundational to your life, and I can only touch on it here. Not only are you saved, you have authority over the darkness.

[6]   Romans 6:3–6

His feet, and gave Him to be head over all things to the church, which is His body, the fullness of Him who fills all in all.

—*Ephesians 1:19–23 (italics added)*

Our elevated spiritual position in Christ is at God's right hand. We are no longer beneath (or subject to) these forces. We are above them, seated with Christ on His throne. Our body may be here on earth, but in our born-again spirit we are seated with Him *positionally* and *spiritually.* That means the authority of Christ, originating at God's right hand, operates through us over the demonic realm within the sphere of our influence. The enemy is beneath our feet. Even if we are the little toe of the left foot of His body, we are still seated in heavenly places in Christ![7]

But God, who is rich in mercy, because of His great love with which He loved us, even when we were dead in trespasses, made us alive together with Christ (by grace you have been saved), *and raised us up together, and made us sit together in the heavenly places in Christ Jesus…*
—*Ephesians 2:4–6 (italics added)*

Heavenly Father, thank You for raising me with Christ to a position at Your right hand. Seated in Him, I am near enough to whisper my prayers in Your ear. You are near enough to assure me of Your presence. I am blessed in Christ and don't have to put up with demonic insults. I have the right to command the enemy away from my life, my family, and my household in Jesus' name. As I pray in faith, my path is prepared before my family and me. Thank You for giving us power over those things that hinder Your work and kingdom, in Jesus' name. Amen.

---

[7] These are deep concepts that may take years to wrap our minds around. Our spirit will understand, but it may take time for our understanding to catch up. When a new thought goes over my head—and it's happened many times—I put it on the shelf, so to speak, and come back to it another time.

Binding and loosing with the keys of the Kingdom

Jesus knew His authority would be transferred to the Church. Therefore, He declared that the gates of hell would not be able to prevail against it. Further, He promised to give us the keys of the kingdom of heaven, the keys of binding and loosing. As Christ's disciples, we have the right to bind and loose in the second heaven.

> "And I also say to you that you are Peter, and on this rock I will build My church, and the gates of Hades shall not prevail against it. And I will give you *the keys of the kingdom of heaven,* and whatever you bind on earth will be bound in heaven, and whatever you loose on earth will be loosed in heaven."
>
> —*Matthew 16:18–19 (italics added)*

Keys represent authority, the right to bind or loose, lock or unlock, forbid or permit. Everyone desires to prevent evil from happening, and this passage gives us great hope. But how do we use these keys?

First, we have to *believe* that we really have power to bind and loose. When I was young in the Lord, I could quote the above Scripture, but I didn't act like I believed it. In my heart I still thought that as soon as heaven (God) bound the problem, it would be bound on earth. Since I was failing to exercise my authority in Christ, I would pray and continue to struggle.

But Jesus said, "And whatever *you* bind on earth will be bound in heaven." However, I did not feel worthy, qualified, or powerful enough to bind anything spiritual, especially creepy things I could not see, so I stood in faith for the Lord to do the binding for me. But that's not the way it works. Jesus transferred His authority to *us.* In His name, *we* must first bind on earth, and then it will be bound in heaven.

While I was a new Christian, others prayed for me, and I experienced many dramatic breakthroughs even though I personally did not bind or loose. But as I became older, others' prayers no longer had the same effect. It was time for me to pray for myself.

For example, after my mother taught me to tie my shoes, I still fussed in a vain attempt to get her to do it for me. She refused and held her ground, and I've been tying my own shoes ever since. It's the same way with binding and loosing. Once you've learned to bind and loose, you need to do it for yourself and not make a fuss for God or someone else to do it for you. (Yes, sometimes you need reinforcements, but not every day.) As you mature in your spiritual authority, you'll be able to pray for the young ones who don't yet know how to pray for themselves.

> *…the authority of Christ, originating at God's right hand, operates through us over the demonic realm within the sphere of our influence. The enemy is beneath our feet!*

We have been given the right to speak into the spiritual atmosphere of the second heaven and "bind" the demons coming against us. We do the speaking on earth in Jesus' name, trusting God's Word, and God and the angels do the binding in the second heaven. We also have the right to "loose" the Holy Spirit's grace, freedom, love, joy, peace, and protection.

While many understand the words "binding and loosing" in the sense of "forbidding and permitting" (such as the exercise of church authority by the Jerusalem council of Acts 15), the meaning of Jesus' words is not limited to the exercise of organizational authority. Only I can forbid or permit things of a personal nature to inhabit my spiritual atmosphere and that of my family. I have the right to command what is not of God to leave in Jesus' name.

Purifying our spiritual atmosphere

Jesus employed the keys of the kingdom to take charge of His spiritual atmosphere. In Matthew 4:10, He ordered Satan to get away from Him: "Away with you, Satan! For it is written, 'You shall worship the LORD your God, and Him only you shall serve.'" In His name we can do the same.

Jesus did not allow His spiritual atmosphere to be polluted by evil spirits any more than you want the wrong people hanging around your children. We purify our space by *commanding* those things that work iniquity to depart from us. (Please be more diplomatic with people.)

Jesus quoted David, saying, *"Depart from Me, all you workers of iniq-uity!"*[8] It's so much easier to live as a Christian in clean air.

Jesus spoke many parables about the great separation of the last days, when He separates wheat from tares, good fish from bad fish, and sheep from goats.[9] When He judges the nations, He will order the sheep to stand on His right hand and the goats on His left. Then He will command those on His left, "Depart from Me…"

> ### As a "royal priesthood," God gave us the right to pray like a priest and command like a king.

Without taking anything away from this glimpse of future judgment, Jesus revealed a helpful principle—we can purge our "heavens" like He did. We use the keys of the kingdom to bind and loose through our words of command.

Many years ago, I was given these prayers to purify my atmosphere.

> *Let all unclean, impure, and unholy spirits depart from me, in the name of Jesus.*
>
> *All spirits that are not Christians, called by that name and walking that path, depart from me, in Jesus' name. You will not inhabit my body, and you will not inhabit my mind.*

Honestly, for a season, I spent too much time binding and rebuking things. As I matured, I learned to keep my eyes focused on Jesus and not on the dark side. Lighting a candle is more effective than cursing the darkness. Nevertheless, our Lord trusts us with great spiritual authority in His name, and we need to use it to command evil forces away from us and our families.

---

[8]   Luke 13:27, Psalm 6:8
[9]   Matthew 13:24–30, 36–43, 47–48, 25:31–46

"Jehovah and Sons/Daughters, Inc."

We bind and loose *by faith* in our partnership with God. When we speak a command on earth to bind something, we *trust* it will be bound in the second heaven. We believe the Lord and the holy angels will back us up by binding the demons. We are Christ's disciples, purchased by His blood, having the mind of Christ and the right to use His name. We operate as sons and daughters of God *in partnership with God.* To move in this kind of faith, we must be guided by the Holy Spirit.

While young, Jesus was the apprentice of his earthly father Joseph, the carpenter. At the same time, He was also the apprentice of His heavenly Father, the Carpenter of Creation.

> Then Jesus answered and said to them, "Most assuredly, I say to you, the Son can do nothing of Himself, but what He sees the Father do; for whatever He does, the Son also does in like manner. For the Father loves the Son, and shows Him all things that He Himself does; and He will show Him greater works than these, that you may marvel."
>
> —*John 5:19–20*

God desires for us, as maturing sons and daughters, to learn wisdom by spending time with Him and seeing what He does. We do not know everything, so as we step out in faith to do what Jesus did, the Holy Spirit teaches us wisdom. A father always knows when it's time to give the keys of the car to a trusted son or daughter trained by him.

Jesus has done everything He is going to do about the devil. He won the decisive victory, obtained our right standing with God, disarmed principalities and powers,[10] filled us with the Holy Spirit, gave us His authority, and empowered us to do the works He did. Now we must learn to use the authority He shared with us in His name to defeat the spiritual resistance hindering the gospel.

Though there are gaps in our knowledge and we need much grace, the Holy Spirit is here to guide us. The keys of binding and loosing are to be used in company with the Lord, and we are not expected to do these things apart from Him.

---

[10]   Colossians 2:15

We use our authority to purify our lives first. Then we intercede for those around us. Intercessors often discern things they cannot share but pray about in secret. In this way, they do not offend those who might misunderstand a vocalized prayer to bind a demonic influence.

Pray like a priest, command like a king

Jesus gave us power to cast out demons and promised that nothing shall by any means hurt us. Like Him, we must stand against evil. Our job is to "speak to the mountain." God's job is to back us up and cause it to move. Our authority does not extend over other peoples' free will, but we can prayerfully (silently) rebuke the ungodly spiritual forces influencing their poor choices. Are you willing to grow into the man or woman of God Jesus died for you to become? Ready or not, we are partners with the Lord. *As a "royal priesthood," God gave us the right to pray like a priest and command like a king.*

Your faith in Jesus Christ makes you a partaker of His victory. The key battle has already been won. Today, you don't fight *for* victory—you fight *from* victory. As a born-again child of God, the Spirit of Christ's victory lives big in you. Just as Jesus refused to be a slave to bad habits, addictions, and attitudes, you also long to be free because *His* Spirit now lives in you.

Through the ultimate showdown, Jesus restored man's original authority and dominion, but none of that is accessible until we enter a covenant relationship with Him. In the next chapter, we'll look at the life of Abraham and see how to make covenant with God, so we can live in the light of His protection.

SECRET #1: Having defeated Satan decisively and eternally, Jesus gave you who believe the authority to command evil spirits to depart from you and your family in His matchless name!

CHAPTER TWO

God's Covenant of Protection

And if you are Christ's, then you are Abraham's seed,
and heirs according to the promise. —*Galatians 3:29*

Abram climbed to the top of the mountain for the second time that day and scanned the horizon. He saw no clouds of dust or glints of armor in the light of the setting sun. Nothing but stillness, a gentle breeze, and a few birds chirping. As he descended to camp, his steward returned from the village where Abram had sent him, not so much for supplies but for any news.

"What's the latest?" Abram asked.

"Just local gossip. No word of troops nearby."

"Say nothing to Sarai or the women," Abram replied as he assigned lookouts for the night.

Abram in the Bible (later renamed Abraham by the Lord) was a spiritual man, a man of peace, right? I always assumed so. But a few days before this conversation might have taken place, he heard his nephew Lot had been captured. So he assembled three friends and three hundred and eighteen of his own men, and with this tiny force led a commando-style, nighttime raid against the joint forces of four powerful Middle Eastern kings and rescued his nephew.[1]

Abram routed the armies, freed the captives, and recovered the invaders' loot. On his return, he offered ten per cent of the spoils (the

---

[1] Genesis 14:8–24

tithe) to the Lord in care of Melchizedek, the priest and king of Salem, a nearby village destined to become Jerusalem. Melchizedek was also a believer in the one true God and a type of Jesus Christ. He brought out bread and wine for a sacred meal and blessed Abram.

Going home with Melchizedek's blessing in the silence after the storm, Abram stayed vigilant. He surveyed the horizon by day and lay awake at night, listening for the sound of horses and soldiers coming in retaliation for his daring attack. Then God appeared and did for him what He hadn't done for any man, making him a solemn promise of protection.

> After these things the word of the LORD came to Abram in a vision, saying, *"Do not be afraid, Abram. I am your shield, your exceedingly great reward."*
>
> —*Genesis 15:1 (italics added)*

Divine protection is an important theme in Scripture, and we'll learn more about it in this chapter and the rest of this book.

God is our shield

The Lord quieted Abram's fear and promised to protect him, saying, *"I…am your shield."* He did not say, "I will give you a shield," but *"I am your shield."* *God Himself* was the shield. Abram relaxed as he put his trust in God's first recorded promise of protection. When the Almighty is our Protector, we sleep in peace because He is near and never sleeps.[2] What a blessing to place our life and the lives of those we love into God's faithful hands! This first mention of protection in the Bible establishes the pattern for future references.

God further promised to be Abram's *"exceedingly great reward."* The reward of faith is personally knowing the Lord—the kindest, wisest, most righteous, and most compassionate Person in existence. Heaven is where we'll live in God's presence forever, and what a joy that will be! Material things and pleasures of this life can never compare to the eternal reward of knowing God and experiencing the exquisite joys of His love for us as individuals.

---

[2]   Psalm 121:4

The faith spoken of around the world

A few verses after God's promise, we find the most talked about example of faith in the Bible. Abram desired a son, and his wife Sarai (whom the Lord renamed Sarah) couldn't have children. But then God promised Abram descendants as numerous as the stars. This amazing God-moment changed Abram's future, and he responded in faith.

> Then He brought him [Abram] outside and said, "Look now toward heaven, and count the stars if you are able to number them." And He said to him, "So shall your descendants be." *And he believed in the LORD, and He accounted it to him for righteousness.*
> —Genesis 15:5–6 (italics added)

Abram's faith was not blind but established on something tangible—God's spoken Word, "So shall your descendants be." He based his faith not on a feeling but on what God said. This pleased the Lord, and He accounted Abram's faith the same as living a righteous life.[3]

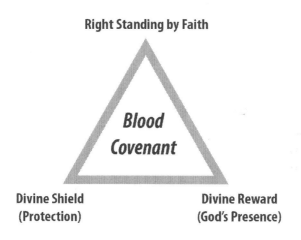

Right Standing by Faith

Blood Covenant

Divine Shield (Protection)   **Divine Reward (God's Presence)**

The Gospel preached to Abraham.

---

3 This passage is the foundation for the New Testament teaching "justification by faith." Hebrews 11:6, Romans 4:1–3, 4:20–5:1

Paul said the gospel was preached beforehand to Abraham,[4] and in this passage three elements of good news are present: right standing with God through faith, divine protection, and God Himself being the believer's exceedingly great reward.

A sacred blood covenant with God

The Lord then promised to give Abram the land of Israel. Abram asked how he could be sure this would come to pass, and the Lord confirmed the promises by making a *blood covenant*[5] with him through which He vowed to fulfill them. A covenant ceremony sealed with blood is the most solemn, sacred agreement possible because one pledges his life as the guarantee. In ancient days, covenant partners vowed: "May my life become as the life of these animals, whose blood has been shed, if I do not fulfill the terms of this covenant."

What amazes me is that the Lord initiated the covenant. He came to Abram, not the other way around. The Lord promised to be a God to Abraham and his descendants, and they would be His people.[6] In so doing, He revealed the attributes of His love, goodness, and faithfulness. This covenant had such profound implications that it impacted the role angels would play as helpers to God's people, as we'll see in Chapter Five. Throughout the history of Israel, God demonstrated protection to His covenant people as they walked in obedience to Him.

The Old Testament is filled with dozens of references to the Lord's protection. The Hebrew words *samar* and *nasar* are often translated "keep," "preserve," "watch over," and "guard." The Aaronic blessing, for example, which the priests pronounced over Israel, contains the word *samar*, which means "guard."

> "The LORD bless you and *keep* [*samar*, guard] you;
> The LORD make His face shine upon you,
> And be gracious to you;
> The LORD lift up His countenance upon you,
> And give you peace."
>   —*Numbers 6:24–26 (italics added)*

---

[4]   Galatians 3:8
[5]   Genesis 15:7-21
[6]   Genesis 17:7

Abraham's covenant of blessing applied to him, his children, and his children's children. The blessing passed to Isaac, to Jacob (also known as Israel), and then to the children of Israel down through the centuries.

Our modern culture with its fear of commitment may struggle to understand the primitive force of a blood covenant, where each party vows loyalty—even to death. Keeping a covenant in ancient times was a matter of personal honor. Marriage to this day is a *covenant* relationship, not a contract. Being true to your covenant means walking in faithfulness, loyalty, and love, holding back nothing from your spouse. Mankind has not always been faithful to their covenants, but the Lord is faithful to His. He is still our shield and eternal reward.

The new covenant shield

However, perhaps you are thinking, "It's sure wonderful that God blessed Abraham and the Jewish people, but how do the promises made to them apply to me?" Here's how Paul explained it:

> For you are all sons of God through faith in Christ Jesus. For as many of you as were baptized into Christ [Abraham's seed or descendant] have put on Christ. ... And if you are *Christ's,* then *you* are Abraham's seed [descendant], and heirs according to the promise.
> —*Galatians 3:26–27, 29 (italics added)*

> Christ has redeemed us from the curse of the law, having become a curse for us (for it is written, "Cursed is everyone who hangs on a tree"), that *the blessing of Abraham might come upon the Gentiles in Christ Jesus,* that we might receive the promise of the Spirit through faith.
> —*Galatians 3:13–14 (italics added)*

By faith in Jesus, we are sons of God and joint-heirs with Christ of Abraham's blessing, including God's promise to be our shield. More than any man, Christ fully inherited the blessing of Abraham. When we are in Him, the full blessing comes on us.

God is serious about His covenant

Years after the covenant was made, the Lord asked Abraham to offer his dearly beloved son Isaac on the altar. Because Abraham loved God enough to do this, another Father offered His beloved Son Jesus Christ on the same mountain centuries later in covenant exchange. When Jesus went to the cross, shed His blood, and offered His life, God ratified the new covenant. This time it was not made with the blood of animals but with the blood of His Son Jesus. Plus, He made the new covenant available to everyone who believes in Jesus, regardless of race, gender, or status of life.

Imagine if God came down from heaven and made a personal blood covenant with you. How would that make you feel? Do you realize He has already done so in the person of Jesus? Will He honor His covenant with you, sealed in the blood of Christ? Of course, He will. Unlike man, God never changes. He is loyal, committed, and utterly trustworthy, saying:

> "My covenant I will not break,
>   Nor alter the word that has gone out of My lips."
>
> —*Psalm 89:34*

Both His covenant and Word are reliable and true. In 2 Corinthians 6:16, He says, "I will be their God, and they shall be My people."

New Testament promises of protection

Though we in the church usually focus on the forgiveness of sins, the new covenant also includes protection and the promises of God's personal presence through the Holy Spirit. The New Testament contains many pledges of blessing and safety. Jesus and the apostles taught about protection through such words as *keep, guard, preserve,* and *deliver.* These come from the Greek roots *tereo, phulasso, phroureo,* and others.

> "Now I am no longer in the world, but these are in the world, and I come to You. Holy Father, *keep* [*tereo*] through Your name those whom You have given Me, that they may be one as We are."
>
> —*John 17:11 (italics added)*

> "I do not pray that You should take them out of the world, but that You should *keep* [*tereo*] them from the evil one."
>
> —*John 17:15 (italics added)*

Paul and the others spoke of the protection that belongs to believers.

And the peace of God, which surpasses all understanding, will *guard* [*phroureo*] your hearts and minds through Christ Jesus.
—*Philippians 4:7 (italics added)*

Now may the God of peace Himself sanctify you completely; and may your whole spirit, soul, and body be *preserved* [*tereo*] blameless at the coming of our Lord Jesus Christ.
—*1 Thessalonians 5:23 (italics added)*

But the Lord is faithful, who will establish you and *guard* [*phulasso*] you from the evil one.
—*2 Thessalonians 3:3 (italics added)*

And the Lord will *deliver* [*rhuomai*] me from every evil work and *preserve* [*sozo*] me for His heavenly kingdom. To Him be glory forever and ever. Amen!
—*2 Timothy 4:18 (italics added)*

Who are *kept* [*phroureo*] by the power of God through faith for salvation ready to be revealed in the last time.
—*1 Peter 1:5 (italics added)*

To those who are called, sanctified by God the Father, and *preserved* [*tereo*] in Jesus Christ:
—*Jude :1 (italics added)*

Now to Him who is able to *keep* [*phulasso*] you from
  stumbling,
And to present you faultless
Before the presence of His glory with exceeding joy,
To God our Savior,
Who alone is wise,
Be glory and majesty,
Dominion and power,
Both now and forever. Amen.
—*Jude 24–25 (italics added)*

In exchange for His covenant love and protection, what does God ask? *All of ourselves! Absolute surrender! Our loyalty! Our obedience!* To give less to such an amazing Partner would be an insult. We respond by making ourselves available to the Lord for His uses and purposes. When He needs to deliver a smile, we are His face. When He needs to extend a helping hand, we are His hands. When He needs to convey a message of love, we are His feet.

How you can enter God's covenant of protection

Suppose you are invited to a wedding and drive to the venue. If you do not enter and sign the guest book, you will not partake of the festivities. You will not see the joy of the bride, share the wedding meal, or taste the wedding cake. Why? Not because you weren't invited, but because you would not walk through the door.

God has given everyone an invitation to enter the covenant of blessing, but the offer must be accepted to become effective. If you have not welcomed Jesus into your heart as Lord and Savior, you have yet to inherit the promises of right standing with God, divine protection, and reward. You are standing outside the door of the wedding covenant, and God's blessings and benefits cannot be enjoyed.

"Do not be afraid... I am your shield, your exceedingly great reward!"

The Father loves and invites all, but we must walk through the Door,[7] who is Jesus Christ, to enjoy the wedding feast He has prepared. The Lord doesn't show favoritism or exclude anyone, regardless of past behavior, gender, ethnic origin, or economic status. (Whew!) The ground is level at the foot of the cross. When you humbly ask Jesus to come into your heart and make a covenant with you, He will.

The good news is "God so loved the world that He gave His only begotten Son, that whoever believes in Him should not perish but have everlasting life."[8] Jesus bore the penalty of our sins, suffering in His own body the punishment you and I deserved. But God raised Him from the dead the third day, free from sin, as proof of our forgiveness.[9] Jesus did not come to condemn the world[10] but to set us free forever from guilt and condemnation, so we can experience deep soul-peace with God.

---

[7] John 10:7, 9
[8] John 3:16
[9] Romans 4:25 (NKJV)
[10] John 3:17–19

It's easy to enter the covenant of protection by accepting Jesus as your Savior. Here's a simple prayer anyone can pray. If you have walked away from the Lord, your relationship can be instantly restored by recommitting yourself in prayer.

> *Lord Jesus, I believe in my heart that You are God's Son. You died bearing the penalty of my sins, so that I may have a new beginning and a fresh start. I repent of my sins and ask for forgiveness and cleansing. I receive You now as my Savior and Lord. I accept the free gift of Your righteousness, which means I am now right with God and completely forgiven. Come into my heart, make me a new creation, and fill me with your Holy Spirit. Thank You for reconciling me to the Father and making me a child of God with the seed of His greatness planted in my heart. Thank You for divine protection and an eternal home in heaven when I die. In Jesus' name, I pray. Amen.*

If you opened your heart to Jesus and prayed that prayer, you are born again[11] and eligible for God's best blessings, including forgiveness, divine protection, and a home in heaven. You are now reconnected to God as your Father and no longer an "orphan spirit," struggling, alone, and without a spiritual Father. As you draw near to Him, God becomes the loving Father you may never have had. His resources are yours, and He will be a God to you. You are His child, a child of the one true King.

By trusting Jesus, you become a member of the Church, those who believe Jesus is the Messiah. The Church is precious to God and called the bride, the Lamb's wife.[12] As a husband cherishes and protects his wife, so the Lord cares for and defends His Church. He wraps his everlasting arms around her. No matter what comes against her, He gave His Word that no one can snatch her out of His omnipotent hands.[13]

Receiving Christ is a power transaction. If you made a mutual defense treaty with an ally, you would expect him to move his assets into a position where he could defend you. Likewise, He would expect you to

---

[11] John 3:3–6
[12] Revelation 21:9, Isaiah 54:5, Hosea 2:19–20
[13] John 10:28–29

be ready to defend him. If you want God involved in your defense, make a covenant with Him now by accepting the free gift of Jesus as your Savior. What do you have to lose? When you do, He shifts resources into place to protect you. This doesn't mean you'll never face trouble or be tested, but that God and Jesus will never leave you nor forsake you. They will guard and strengthen you, no matter what you face, and at your last day on earth take you to your eternal home in heaven.

Find safety under the umbrella of your covenant with the Lord.

Like Abraham and Jesus, you too can live in the light and protection of a covenant with God, which includes forgiveness of sins and the protective ministry of angels. However, before we can move on and talk more about angels, we need to lay some groundwork first and take a biblical look at what it means to thrive in the light of Jesus.

SECRET #2: To walk in divine protection, you must make a covenant with God through faith in Jesus Christ, through which you receive forgiveness of sins, right standing with God, peace, protection, and eternal reward. You enter the covenant when you personally invite Jesus to be your Savior and Lord.

CHAPTER THREE

Living in the Light

*But the path of the righteous is like the light of dawn, which
shines brighter and brighter until full day. —Proverbs 4:18 (ESV)*

The number one way to scatter the darkness and live in the light of
Christ is to fill our minds with God's Word. The entrance of God's
Word gives light, and light penetrates, repels, and overcomes the darkness.

> Your word is *a lamp* to my feet
> And *a light* to my path.
>
> —*Psalm 119:105 (italics added)*

> *The entrance of Your words gives light;*
> It gives understanding to the simple.
>
> —*Psalm 119:130 (italics added)*

As we follow Jesus and receive His words, we have the light of life.

Our new birth is like the original creation

It fascinates me that the Christian experience parallels the creation.

> For it is the God who [in the beginning] commanded light to shine
> out of darkness, who has shone in our hearts to give the light of the
> knowledge of the glory of God in the face of Jesus Christ.
>
> —*2 Corinthians 4:6*

In the beginning, darkness was on the face of the deep, and God
said, "Let there be light!" and there was light. Before we came to Christ,

the world had darkened our minds. We lived in spiritual ignorance, no matter how much worldly education we had. Paul described our pre-saved condition clearly.

> So I tell you this, and insist on it in the Lord, that you must no lon-ger live as the Gentiles do, in the futility of their thinking. They are *darkened in their understanding* and *separated from the life of God* because of the *ignorance* that is in them due to the *hardening of their hearts.*
>
> —*Ephesians 4:17–18 (NIV, italics added)*

A hardened heart that doesn't acknowledge the Lord is the cause of spiritual ignorance, and that darkened understanding *separates* a per-son from the life of God. In that state, we are separated from the good things that come from God—love, joy, peace, faith, creativity, innova-tion, kindness, and so forth. To be cut off from the life of God is to live a dull and colorless life.

We paid a huge price in our pre-Christian life for a hardened heart. Our lack of understanding imposed a barrier that prevented us from experiencing God's forgiveness, presence, protection, wisdom, love, joy, and peace. But when we accepted Jesus as Savior, His light entered and exposed the darkness for what it was. As we followed Him, His light began to overcome the darkness in us.

But the Lord didn't stop with saying, "Let there be light," He did something more—*He separated the light from the darkness!* As His chil-dren, we imitate Him and drive the darkness out of ourselves by strong infusions of the light of His Word. The Lord wants us filled with light, so that His light not only shines on us, it shines *in* us and *through* us.

> "Make sure that the light you think you have is not actually dark-ness. If you are filled with light, with no dark corners, then your whole life will be radiant, as though a floodlight were filling you with light."
>
> —*Luke 11:35–36 (NLT)*

Worshiping Him who is light

As we lift our hearts to the Lord in worship, we focus on Him who is light, and His light floods into our souls. When I was a kid, I used a magnifying glass to focus the sunlight and burn holes in paper. One time the paper burst into flames. As we magnify the Lord in worship, we focus His radiance within us until our heart catches fire. Through worship and the Word, we absorb the life (energy) and light (wisdom) to overcome life's challenges.

The principle of the single (or good) eye applies here.[1] Whatever we set our heart's affection on is what floods into our souls. When we focus on worldly things—career, goals, material possessions, food and drink, entertainment, vacations, and pleasures—that's what fills our hearts. So, we must make sure that the "light" in us is not actually darkness. However, when we focus on the Lord, He fills our hearts with the light of life that carries with it all His benefits.

An illuminated spirit and a darkened soul

When you and I were born again, a new day dawned. The depressing darkness of night was replaced with the colorful hues of a Son-drenched morning. In new birth, the Lord re-created and illuminated our *spirits* (hearts) instantly, but He did not transform our *souls* (mind, will, and emotions). That's why we woke up the day after we were saved and wondered if salvation was real, because our soul was still the same.

A newly born-again child of God has an illuminated spirit with a dark and worldly soul. Yes, we truly experienced salvation and forgiveness, but we find ourselves thinking like the world, making decisions like the world, and reacting emotionally like the world. This is a strange state of being: our hearts desire to do what is right before God, but our souls tend to act as we always have.

We have no doubt that the miracle done in our *spirit* is the workmanship of God.[2] So, if there is a problem, it's not in our *spirit*, but in the *soul*, in our intellect, emotions, and will. In the last half of Romans 7, Paul described the double-mindedness we experience. We have the best of intentions for doing right but often fail to do as we intend. God did a wonderful work when we said Yes to Jesus, but now *we* must accept our responsibility and compel our walk to line up with our talk.

---

[1]   Matthew 6:22–23
[2]   Ephesians 2:10

Living in the light is a choice

So, what does it take to live in the light? Spiritual illumination filled our *spirit* as God refathered us, making us partakers of His divine nature and spiritual DNA.[3] But now it is only by our *free-will choices* that we give the light entrance into our mind, will, and emotions.

To be filled with light, we must *choose* the light and *focus* intently on the light. As the eye focuses on the subject of its gaze, we are filled with the light of Christ when we turn our *full concentration* to the Lord and His Word. We must *love* the light of God's truth over everything else if we wish to be delivered from the lying deceptions of the evil one.[4] Living in the light doesn't happen automatically just because we are Christians— *it's a lifestyle choice!*

> For you were once darkness, but now you are light in the Lord. *Live as children of light* (for the fruit of the light consists in all goodness, righteousness and truth) and find out what pleases the Lord. Have nothing to do with the fruitless deeds of darkness, but rather expose them. It is shameful even to mention what the disobedient do in secret. But everything exposed by the light becomes visible—and everything that is illuminated becomes a light. This is why it is said: "Wake up, sleeper, rise from the dead, and Christ will shine on you."
> —*Ephesians 5:8–14 (NIV, italics added)*

Perhaps you've noticed that God does not force you to read His Word, attend church or small groups, or go to conferences where the light-filled Word of God is preached, even though those things are good for you. That choice is yours.

Sadly, as born-again Christians, when we don't fill ourselves with light on a regular basis, we become spiritually unfruitful. If we don't spend enough time in light-filled environments, we can't absorb the truth of who we are in Christ and discover our divine purpose. When we don't grow "roots" into the light and draw nourishment from the river of living water, we can't bear mature fruit. The "trouble or persecution" we

---

[3]   2 Peter 1:4
[4]   2 Thessalonians 2:10 (9–12)

face, the "stony places" in our hearts, and the "thorns" of this world's distractions choke our seed from producing a harvest.[5]

It requires an *inward, forcible revolution* to become Jesus' disciple and follow in His footsteps.[6] Why? Because God is a perfect gentleman and gives freedom of choice to all. He won't compel anyone to renew their mind, surrender their will, or purify their emotions. It's *our job,* not God's, to break out of conformity to this world and choose the light of His Word over the dark ways to which we are accustomed.

The secret of spiritual transformation

Paul told us plainly how to grow and mature in Christ. The *only* way to be transformed is by the renewing of our minds, by planting the light-filled thoughts of Scripture into our minds and hearts abundantly. Paul wrote:

> I beseech you therefore, brethren, by the mercies of God, that you present your bodies a living sacrifice, holy, acceptable to God, which is your reasonable service. And do not be conformed to this world, but *be transformed by the renewing of your mind,* that you may prove what is that good and acceptable and perfect will of God.
>
> —*Romans 12:1–2 (italics added)*

Speaking to those in the church, the apostle tells us there is something *saved* people must do with their bodies and their minds. We are...

(1) *To present our bodies as living sacrifices.*

(2) *To be transformed by the renewing of our minds.*

But who must do this, God or us? He said, "...*you* present your bodies," and *[you]* "be transformed by the renewing of your mind."

(1) *We* must offer our bodies as living sacrifices to God. After offering them, we are to reckon our bodies now dead—dead people don't sin![7]—and crucify the sinful desires of the flesh.

(2) As if that weren't enough, *we* are to stop thinking like a dark world and acquire new and godly thoughts from Scripture. The New Living Translation translates Romans 12:2 like this, "Don't copy the

---

[5] Matthew 13:5–7, 20–22

[6] Matthew 11:12

[7] Romans 6:11–12

behavior and customs of this world, but let God transform you into a new person by changing the way you think."

We are to acquire the "mind of Christ," having the same thoughts, priorities, and attitudes Jesus Christ had.[8] While that sounds unattainable, it *can* be achieved (as much as humanly possible) by focusing on God's Word as the only reliable guide for truth and living.

Paul told us what to do with our bodies and minds, but notice he didn't tell us what to do with our spirit. Why? Because what happened in our born-again spirit is the workmanship of God, and that can't be improved on, only nourished and stirred up.

Beliefs control actions

You've probably observed, like I have, that people give lip service to many things but act according to what they really believe. A core belief precedes and determines action. So, if we want to change our actions, we must first change our fundamental beliefs about God. We need to know how much He loves us, who we are in Him, and why we are here. We are changed according to how much of His light penetrates our minds and hearts.

We must be *willing* to hear from the Lord. Jesus said we need "ears to hear," ears that hunger to receive and understand His Word.[9] So, if we refuse to read the Word of God regularly, put our hands over our ears when it makes us uncomfortable, or fill our lives so full of worldly stuff we don't have time for Him, the result becomes obvious. We can't and don't change, our spiritual growth is stunted, and we end up not fulfilling our divine purpose.

For example, when Martha complained to Jesus that Mary wasn't helping her in the kitchen, she thought He would surely command her sister to start helping. Instead, Jesus commended Mary for sitting at His feet and receiving His Word.[10] The Word of God is light-giving for the spirit and soul (higher priority) while the kitchen is necessary for the body.

Positive changes take place when the Bible's truths are planted in our hearts and replace the devil's lies. As our beliefs change, our actions

---

[8]   Philippians 2:5
[9]   Matthew 13:19
[10] Luke 10:41–42

change as well. A foundation built on the bedrock of hearing and doing Christ's Word stands secure, so we are neither moved nor destroyed by the storms of life.[11]

> *But the Lord didn't stop with saying, "Let there be light," He did something more— He separated the light from the darkness! As His children, we are to imitate Him and drive the darkness out of ourselves by strong infusions of the light of His Word.*

The Bible is the treasure house of God's thoughts, which are new thoughts and new "seed." As we meditate in His Word, we plant this seed into the garden of our mind and heart. As the seed germinates and grows, it changes our beliefs and behavior. The more of the Word we plant, understand, and act on, the quicker our transformation.

But until we put the new thoughts of God into our minds, we continue to live by the old (worldly) thoughts by which we've always lived. We do the same things over and over, hoping for different results but never getting them. The Bible declares we are transformed, matured, and changed *only* by the renewing of our minds.

Transfigured by the light of God's Word

The word "transformed" in Romans 12:2 comes from the Greek verb *metamorphoo,* the root of our word *metamorphosis.* Metamorphosis is that amazing process in which a caterpillar eats until it can eat no more, spins a weird-looking chrysalis around itself, and miraculously emerges days later as a butterfly.

Metamorphoo is the word used in Scripture to describe the *transfiguration* of Jesus, as He was transformed into a brilliant and glorious state before the amazed eyes of Peter, James, and John.[12] When we realize the idea of transfiguration is implied also in Romans 12:2, we get a better

---

[11] Matthew 7:24–27
[12] Matthew 17:2, Mark 9:2–3

understanding of all the Holy Spirit is saying. *We are transfigured on the inside into the glorious, light-radiating image of Christ through the renewing of our minds.*[13]

God has given us a born-again spirit, but for us to grow up in Christ He needs our whole-hearted and willing cooperation. Will you commit today to becoming a "Word person," who meditates in God's Word day and night, allowing His life-transforming light into your soul? You will become like a tree planted by rivers of living water that bears its fruit in its season.[14] Your leaf also will not wither, and whatever you do will prosper, because you live in the light of God's Word.

Our light-filled identity is derived from the Word

Every Christian I know cherishes specific Scriptures that have enlightened and radically changed their lives. What God says about us in His Word is so much higher and better than what we think of ourselves. We are transformed as we discover who He declared us to be in Christ.

God made us in His image, but since the Fall our inner image has been shaped by what others have said over us, such as parents, teachers, friends, enemies, spouses, ex-spouses, in-laws, out-laws, and so forth. Some spoke well, and we were encouraged. But others spoke evil over us and imprisoned our identity in a box made by their words, as if they were God (and they are not). As a result, in some areas of life we doubt our own ability, worth, and even likability. That crippling, false identity came because evil words were spoken over us like curses.

But just as evil words distorted our inner image, God's more powerful Word reshapes us into a God-given identity, conformed to the image of Christ. It requires our full attention to discover all that Gods Word says we are in Christ. Why? Because the Word declares who we are and gives us the boldness to step into God's purpose, which is always bigger and more challenging than anything we could think to do.

We are God's beloved children, the apple of His eye. We are strong, victorious, full of life, healthy, and more than conquerors. We are able to do all things in Him, being creative and competent. We are complete in

---

[13] See also 2 Corinthians 3:18 for another instance of *metamorphoo*.

[14] Psalm 1:1–3

Him, lacking nothing. We are above and not beneath, the head and not the tail, successful in all we put our hand to. We are full of wisdom and the fruit of the Spirit and have the gifts of the Spirit to bring glory to God. We know and live out our divine purpose. We are forgiven, washed, cleansed, delivered, and set free. We are filled to overflowing with the Holy Spirit, thanking, praising, and worshiping God. We are blameless and without fault. We are filled with the fullness of God. We are walking in our spiritual inheritance now. We are ambassadors of reconciliation for the King of kings and Lord of lords. We are surrounded by divine protection, have a home in heaven, and walk in God's love.

We live in the light of Christ when we own that new identity rooted in His Word!

> *Heavenly Father, I desire to live in the light of Christ and dedicate myself to becoming a Word person. I'm tired of thinking depressed and negative thoughts about myself. The light of Your Word declares I am more than a conqueror through Him who loves me. I commit this day to meditate in Your Word day and night, that I may be transfigured into the glorious image of Christ.*

In the next chapter, we'll see how important it is to open our spiritual eyes and understand the mysteries of the kingdom of heaven.

SECRET #3: God refathered your spirit when you said Yes to Jesus, but you must allow the brilliant light of His Word to enter your soul, renew your mind, and scatter the worldly darkness. As you plant the new thoughts of God's Word in your heart, your beliefs and behavior change. You acquire the mind of Christ and radiate His love by living and walking in the light of your new identity.

CHAPTER FOUR

Seeing into the Invisible Realm

He answered and said to them, "Because it has been given to you to know the mysteries of the kingdom of heaven, but to them it has not been given." —Matthew 13:11

A few years ago my wife Debbie and I visited Disneyland in southern California. As we walked down Main Street, enjoying the crowds, ambience, and Disney characters, we gave no thought to what was behind the scenes. However, when a ride we were on unexpectedly stopped, we had to exit the car and be guided out. The fantasy of the experience disappeared, and we were face-to-face with the mechanical and electrical equipment that runs everything in the park, even though it's skillfully hidden from view.

Our natural, visible world is similar to Disneyland in that behind the scenes is an invisible dimension that affects our "ride." Prior to Walt Disney and his "imagineers," God created things we cannot see *before* He created the things we can see. Creation has two aspects then—the invisible and the visible.

> By faith we understand that the worlds were framed by the word of God, so that *the things which are seen were not made of things which are visible.*
>
> —Hebrews 11:3 (italics added)

Faith empowers us to see that the universe was created and beautifully coordinated by the power of God's words! He spoke and *the invisible realm gave birth to all that is seen.*

—*Hebrews 11:3 (TPT, italics added)*

For by Him [Christ] all things were created that are in heaven and that are on earth, *visible and invisible,* whether thrones or dominions or principalities or powers. All things were created through Him and for Him.

—*Colossians 1:16 (italics added)*

A divine order in creation

The first verse of the Bible says, "In the beginning God created the heavens and the earth."[1] First He made "the heavens," the invisible, spiritual universe, because the *unseen* parts of creation provide the supporting infrastructure for the *seen.* Then God created matter, the earth, and the visible heavens of sun, moon, and stars. The natural depends on the spiritual for its existence, just as the rides in Disneyland depend on hidden machinery put in place long before any "car" was on the track.

Jesus was the only leader in history who demonstrated power over both the material and spiritual realms. To free us, He raised our awareness of spiritual realities, and it doesn't matter in which century we live.

God created all things with His Word, which He spoke into the most highly charged, creative environment ever. For the Holy Spirit hovered over the face of the waters, waiting for each Word God would speak. When He declared, "Let there be light!" there was light. Every out-breathed syllable launched a flurry of innovative activity that catapulted this natural world out of formless chaos into orderly design.[2] To this day God's Word sustains the natural universe.[3]

---

1 Genesis 1:1
2 Genesis 1:2
3 Hebrews 1:3

Who [Jesus] being the brightness of His glory and the express image of His person, and *upholding all things by the word of His power,* when He had by Himself purged our sins, sat down at the right hand of the Majesty on high…

—*Hebrews 1:3 (italics added)*

However, due to our naturalistic training, most of us see this material world only, which we regard as permanent, while supposing the spiritual realm is less credible. But the opposite is true. God's Word and the spiritual infrastructure of the universe will abide forever, long after this material heaven and earth have passed away.[4] Think of creation like an iceberg: the greater part is unseen, lying beneath the surface, behind the veil of mortal sight.

The "heavens"

The Bible uses the word heaven in several ways. It refers to the sky, where birds fly and clouds drift,[5] and to space, where we find the sun, moon, and stars.[6] These heavens are visible and material, observable and measurable by astronomers.

But heaven also means the invisible realms, including the dwelling place of God and the holy angels—where believers go when they die—and the spiritual places near earth fought over by angels and demons. Though we know little of the invisible "heavenly places,"[7] we are comfortable with sky and space, capable of enjoying the soul-expanding beauty of a clear, starry night, which bears witness to our Creator.

As humans, we struggle with things that cannot be known by our *five physical senses.* Since infancy, our senses have shaped (and limited) our idea of reality. But God has given us an unknown and overlooked instrument to perceive spiritual realities. Your conscious human *spirit* is the real you, the hidden person of your heart.[8] You are a spirit, having a soul (the mind, will, and emotions), living in a body. (You are so much

---

4   Matthew 24:35

5   Genesis 1:6–8

6   Genesis 1:16–17

7   Ephesians 1:3, 20, 2:6, 3:10, 6:12

8   1 Corinthians 2:11, 1 Thessalonians 5:23, 1 Peter 3:4. The human spirit is *conscious,* knowing the things of a man *and* giving life to the body (James 2:26, Luke 8:55).

more than a body with a brain.) Your spirit is sensitive to God and the spiritual realm, being designed for life in two worlds, this one and the world to come.

The Bible describes three "heavens."

Before we became Christians, our spirits were usually dead, blind, and deaf to spiritual things. But as the Holy Spirit drew us to Himself (probably as the result of someone's prayers), our perception of spiritual things increased. We perceived there was more to life than met the natural eye. Today, many feel this inward pull to spiritual things but don't realize it's the love of God drawing them to Christ. At salvation, the Holy Spirit comes to live inside us, and He opens our eyes and ears to spiritual reality.

The three heavens of the Bible

To summarize, the Bible refers to three "heavens," and we'll discuss them in this order—the first, the third, and then the second. The *first heaven* is earth's natural atmosphere, the region of air and clouds where birds fly. It includes what we call "space," the expanding universe of sun, moon, stars, and galaxies beyond galaxies. This visible, natural universe was created by God, who alone made matter out of things unseen, brought forth millions of intricately-designed living creatures from non-living elements, and breathed spirit, consciousness, and personality into man's mortal body.

The amazing place called the *kingdom of heaven,* the *highest heaven,*[9] or the *third heaven,* is located in the highest spiritual realm where God sits enthroned as King.[10] The apostle Paul called the kingdom of heaven the "third heaven."

> I know a man in Christ who fourteen years ago—whether in the body I do not know, or whether out of the body I do not know, God knows—such a one was caught up to the *third heaven.*
> —*2 Corinthians 12:2 (italics added)*

> The LORD has established His throne in heaven,
> And His kingdom rules over all.
> —*Psalm 103:19*

The third heaven is God's home. Nothing disturbs its peace and tranquility because it is separated from all evil. When we talk of dying and going to heaven, it's the third heaven where all is perfect. Here is the City that has foundations, the New Jerusalem, whose builder and maker is God.[11] In the center of the City is God's throne, which both the prophet Daniel and the apostle John saw in their visions.[12]

Invisible to our natural eyes is a spiritual world we do not perceive directly.

God's throne is the "control room" of the universe where the Father reigns over all things, visible and invisible. The hidden, spiritual infrastructure behind everything is joined to the material by invisible links, and these are controlled from His throne. This spiritual technology makes miracles possible. When God chooses, the laws of the material realm are superseded by the laws of the kingdom of heaven.

Since the Bible mentions the natural (first) heaven and the third heaven, there must be a *second heaven* between them. Though the term

---

[9]   Deuteronomy 10:14, Job 22:12

[10] 2 Corinthians 12:2,4, Ephesians 1:3, 20, 2:6

[11] Hebrews 11:10, 16, Revelation 21:1–22:5

[12] Daniel 7:9–10, Revelation 4:2–11, 20:11, 21:5, 22:1, 3

second heaven is not found in the Bible, Paul identified what he called "heavenly places," referring to the *spiritual dimension surrounding earth.*[13] Here God, angels, and demons battle to influence the free-will choices of men and nations. The interaction of the second heaven with our world is a popular theme in television and movies. The Bible describes these heavenly places as the scene of very real spiritual warfare.

> Finally, be strong in the Lord and in his great power. Put on the full armor of God so that you can fight against the devil's evil tricks. Our fight is not against people on earth but against the rulers and authorities and the powers of this world's darkness, against the spiritual powers of evil in the heavenly world.
>
> —*Ephesians 6:10–12 (NCV)*

The mysteries of the kingdom of heaven

> He [Jesus] answered and said to them, "Because it has been given to you *to know the mysteries of the kingdom of heaven,* but to them it has not been given."
>
> —*Matthew 13:11 (italics added)*

Jesus promised to give His disciples an understanding of the mysteries (or invisible workings) of the supreme spiritual realm of all, the kingdom of heaven. He proved His claim that the kingdom of heaven was at hand[14] by demonstrating power over demons and the laws of physics. He walked on water, turned water into wine, healed the sick, raised the dead, and cast out evil spirits.

Although believers enjoy the starlit beauties of the first heaven and are promised eternal life in the third heaven, we dare not be ignorant of the second heaven. From this region we are influenced by powerful personalities—God, Jesus, the Holy Spirit, and holy angels, as well as by the devil and demons.

Personally, I do not like to talk about the devil or give him any credit, but if ignorance was bliss, Jesus, the wisest, kindest Man who ever lived, would have ignored him. Instead, He spoke more about him than any other teacher. He did this to free us from bondage to things we

---

[13] Ephesians 3:10, 6:12

[14] Matthew 4:17

cannot see.[15] Since our Master Teacher thought it important, we must follow His example even if it makes us uncomfortable. The light of the Word of God must be our guide instead of our comfort level.

Superstition versus science

But some insist the idea of a devil is a carryover from man's ignorant, superstitious past and that modern, intelligent people have progressed beyond such primitive concepts. But even if we cured the world's ills and rooted out inequality, racism, and injustice, people and nations would still be tempted to turn to the dark side. Why? Evil exists outside of man in the second heaven, and it is something more than the psychological problems caused by his environment. It is a *spiritual* problem that if not dealt with by faith in Christ causes any culture to unravel and destroy itself from within.

Others assume science disproved the Bible years ago and made the teachings of Jesus irrelevant and obsolete. While today's world prides itself on its scientific achievements and technological advances, and rightfully so, it's vital to recognize one shocking fact—*science and technology are significant only in this material world.* My personal, handheld communication device or any other brilliantly designed machine, whether a space rocket or a life-sustaining medical apparatus, has no value in the spiritual universe. Technology's benefit is limited to this natural, visible world that is passing away. That reminds me of the story of the man who died and reached for his cell phone to get directions to heaven. You need to know where you're going before you die.

Despite its benefits, modern science has not improved the second heaven. So, while man's technical abilities grow by leaps and bounds, giving an illusion of progress, his spiritual condition, influenced by second heaven realities, remains unaffected or has even declined. *The human heart with its often self-centered, prideful, hateful, fearful, greedy, pleasure-driven motives remains unchanged by twenty-first century technology.* That's why we all need to be born again of God.

Only Jesus can take the hard, stony heart out of a man and replace it with a tender heart of flesh, filled with His pure, gracious, generous

---

[15] The Old Testament mentions the devil (also known as Satan) only in five passages, but the New Testament reveals the power of Christ over him and demons dozens of times.

Spirit.[16] Only Jesus can give a man or woman such a selfless spirit that they are willing to sacrifice for others. Jesus came to open our eyes to spiritual realities—*and that's relevant and up-to-date in every century!*

Despite technology, every person struggles with his inner thought life, no matter how many college degrees she has or how artistically or technically educated he is. Greed, pride, lust, manipulation and control, discouragement, depression, despair, and bad thoughts are common to mankind, to gifted musicians and movie stars, to brilliant scientists, to extraordinary athletes, to exceptional businessmen, and to the rest of us.

Troubling thoughts must be dealt with in a healthy and biblical way. A person may be in therapy for years and take a medicine cabinet full of mind-bending pills, but until they come to grips with the *spiritual roots* of the problem, the pain won't go away. Physical solutions can't cure problems rooted in the spiritual realm. Jesus came to enlighten us so we are not destroyed by ignorance of the invisible world.[17]

He gave us powerful weapons to uproot and tear down spiritual strongholds. As we defeat them, we become more joyful, productive, and creative. Our overcoming lives and positive attitudes encourage those around us. And we don't fight alone, for God assigned holy angels to help us, and that is the subject of the next chapter.

> *Heavenly Father, show me the mysteries of the kingdom of heaven. Open my eyes to spiritual realities and train my spirit to know Your presence. Holy Spirit, reveal to me the things about the spiritual realm You want me to know. In Jesus' name, I pray. Amen.*

SECRET #4: A spiritual environment surrounds you. Between God's heaven and earth lies a second heaven, where angels and demons contend for the souls of men. For this reason, natural solutions can't fix problems rooted in the spiritual realm. But in Christ, the kingdom of heaven—the third heaven—gives you authority and power over everything that fights against you in the second heaven.

---

[16] Ezekiel 36:26–27

[17] Hosea 4:6

CHAPTER FIVE

Holy Angels, Your
Heavenly Bodyguards

*The angel of the LORD encamps all around those who fear Him,
And delivers them. —Psalm 34:7*

Years ago, I broke ground for a good-sized vegetable garden. Pausing to take in the sweeping view of the foothills, I became aware of an invisible presence standing beside me. Good or evil? I asked myself.

I lived in the Sierra Nevada mountains east of Fresno, California, and was probably the first person to clear and till that land. Another family had built the modest house but lived there only a short time. Before that? The native Americans of California walked those hills, hunting deer and gathering acorns.

As I stood praying, I sensed how disciplined this being was. He had nerves of steel like a trained warrior, and it seemed he would not move a muscle without a command. Beyond my initial reaction of concern and, I'll admit, a little fear from being in the presence of such a battle-tested combatant, I did not sense evil influencing my mind. After a few minutes, I continued warily about my business.

Nothing bad followed—no bad dreams, no dark thoughts. After replaying this over and over in my mind, I decided God gave me a glimpse into the character of one of the mighty soldiers the Bible calls "angels." In case you don't know, angels are *not* chubby little cherubs playing harps while riding on cotton ball clouds—they are powerful men of war.

The Bible describes angels with different gifts and functions. There are *warring* angels, such as Michael the archangel,[1] *messenger* angels, such as Gabriel,[2] and *worshiping* angels around God's throne.[3] The one I saw delivered no message, so I gathered he was a warring angel, present for my protection. By his intense vigilance, I knew he was on duty to protect me from attacks. He was powerful enough to deal with demons and other things as God commanded him.

Bible history tells us that sometime before the creation of man, Satan rebelled against God. He was present in the Garden of Eden as the serpent, an adversary to man. At some point, one-third of the angels fell from grace, persuaded by the devil to quit doing God's will and follow him, losing their heavenly powers.[4] They were judged, perhaps at the time of the Flood, and some were chained in darkness. However, two-thirds of the angels retained their first estate, showing absolute loyalty to Almighty God, their Maker.

The first recorded instances of angelic help

Adam and Eve were the original guardians of earth, but, unfortunately, they gave the devil legal permission to teach men about evil. As a result, the devil exploited man in his ignorant and sinful state for thousands of years, doing great harm. The devil's influence appears to have been unrestrained before the Flood. The Bible describes that culture as "corrupt before God, and the earth was filled with violence."[5] "...the wickedness of man was great in the earth, and that every intent of the thoughts of his heart was only evil continually."[6] Evidently, few prayed in those days, and the Lord could only intervene in Noah's life.

The existence of angels was known in ancient times, but there is no record in the first two thousand years of earth's history of angels *helping* any human being. The first two thousand years are recorded in Genesis 1–11 and the book of Job.

---

[1] Daniel 10:13, 21, 12:1, Jude :9, Revelation 12:7
[2] Daniel 8:16, 9:21, Luke 1:19, 26
[3] Revelation 5:11–12
[4] Revelation 12:3–4, 2 Peter 2:4-5, Jude :6
[5] Genesis 6:11
[6] Genesis 6:5

Job was a Gentile who lived *before* Abraham and was *not* a partaker of the Abrahamic covenant. Job had no promises made by God to lessen the effects of the Fall. While angels are mentioned in Job 4:18, 5:1, and 38:7 (where they are called "angels," "holy ones," "morning stars," and "sons of God"), nothing suggests they helped or protected Job, either before or after his trial.

> *The existence of angels was known in ancient times, but there is no record in the first two thousand years of earth's history of angels helping any human being.*

For example, Eliphaz asked Job, "Call out now; is there anyone who will answer you? And to which of the *holy ones* will you turn?"[7] He evidently did not believe humanity could receive angelic help. King Nebuchadnezzar, another non-Jewish man without a covenant, called the angels "watchers" and "holy ones."[8] The passive role of angels to those outside the covenants contrasts sharply with the history of Israel and the Church, where they actively help the people of God.

The first reference to a supernatural being other than God occurs in Genesis 3, where Satan, a fallen angel, took the form of a serpent and slithered his way into the Garden of Eden. After man's Fall, God placed cherubim (a supernatural order of winged creatures) at the entrance of the garden of Eden to prevent man from eating of the tree of life.[9]

The first reference to holy angels as we commonly understand them occurs much later. In Chapter Two, we discussed the sacred covenant God made with Abraham recorded in Genesis 15. Interestingly, Genesis 16 begins the long record of angels assisting humans, as the "Angel of the LORD" spoke to Hagar to return and submit to Sarah.[10] In Genesis 19

---

[7] Job 5:1

[8] Daniel 4:13, 17, 23

[9] Genesis 3:24

[10] Genesis 16:7–13, Genesis 19:1, 15, 21:17, 22:11, 15, 24:7, 40, 32:1–2, etc. The One described as the "Angel of the Lord" in Genesis 16:7–13 and other places is often thought to be the Lord Jesus Christ in one of His preincarnate appearances.

two angels helped Lot escape the destruction of Sodom. Could there be a connection between God's covenant and the ministry of angels?

A few decades later, Abraham's grandson Jacob received the "blessing of Abraham" from his father Isaac by the laying on of his hands.[11] Jacob then took his journey to seek a wife. That night he dreamed of a ladder set up on earth that reached to heaven. He saw the angels of God climbing up and down on it while the Lord spoke blessings over him.[12] So, immediately after receiving the covenant blessing from his father, Jacob had a personal encounter with the Lord. His spiritual eyes were opened, and he became aware of holy angels traveling between heaven and earth on his behalf.

If angels had been assisting mankind since the beginning, Jacob's dream is hardly remarkable. But if angels started serving mankind after God made the covenant with Abraham, this was a startling revelation. *The blood covenant made with Abraham and his seed included the protective, helping ministry of angels—perhaps for the first time in human history!* After the covenant was made, angelic appearances are recorded in Genesis, Exodus, Numbers, and Judges. Angels also appeared to King David and the prophets.

Angels in the new covenant

Jesus brought up the subject of angels early in His ministry. He told Nathanael that angels would minister to those who believed He was the Messiah.

> And He said to him, "Most assuredly, I say to you, hereafter you shall see heaven open, and the angels of God ascending and descending upon the Son of Man."
>
> —*John 1:51*

Jesus is "Jacob's Ladder" that was seen centuries before, the connecting bridge between the third heaven and earth, between God and man. Our Lord's presence, even in the Old Testament, made possible the ministry of angels. He is the "seed of Abraham" to whom the covenant

---

[11] Genesis 28:3–4
[12] Genesis 28:10–17

promises were made. Access to the protective power of holy angels comes from entering the new covenant by confessing Jesus as Savior, while denying Him results in being denied before the angels of God.

> "Also I say to you, whoever confesses Me before men, him the Son of Man also will confess before the angels of God. But he who denies Me before men will be denied before the angels of God."
>
> —*Luke 12:8–9*

Jesus spoke these words to an "innumerable multitude"[13] which included opponents as well as disciples. He established a direct link between confessing Him before men (salvation) and Him confessing us before His Father and His angels (protection). He also let it be known that those who publicly deny Him (not in ignorance) would be denied before the angels.

Jesus has existed eternally as the Second Person of the Godhead (prior to His birth in Bethlehem). As the LORD of Hosts, He has always led Heaven's angelic army. When we are in covenant with Jesus, we are protected by the ministry of angels, but if we deny Him we are denied before the angels. Angelic help and spiritual protection belong to those who believe and confess Jesus as Savior and Lord. The writer of the book of Hebrews connected the ministry of angels with salvation:

> Are they not all ministering spirits sent forth to minister for those who will inherit salvation?
>
> —*Hebrews 1:14*

Angels played key roles in establishing the new covenant. An angel spoke to Zacharias, the father of John the Baptist, about John's birth and ministry. The angel Gabriel brought God's Word to Mary that Jesus would be conceived by the Holy Spirit. An angel guided Joseph to take Mary as his wife. Angels praised God at Jesus' birth and sent Joseph and his family into Egypt. Angels ministered to Jesus in His temptation in the wilderness and in the garden of Gethsemane. Angels were present at His resurrection and ascension.

---

[13] Luke 12:1

Angels released the apostles from prison,[14] delivered Peter from prison and execution,[15] and saved Paul from shipwreck and death at sea.[16] The apostle John had an angelic escort in the book of Revelation and saw myriads of angels worshiping and praising God around His throne.[17] Though we may not see them, we are surrounded by angels who stand guard over God's covenant people as part of the shield He promised Abraham. Our physical protection is enhanced by these ministering spirits.[18]

The ministry of angels

The Bible describes the ministry of angels.

> No evil shall befall you,
> Nor shall any plague come near your dwelling;
> For He shall give His angels charge over you,
> To keep you in all your ways.
> In their hands they shall bear you up,
> Lest you dash your foot against a stone.
>
> —*Psalm 91:10–12*

Notice the promise, "No evil shall befall you, nor shall any plague come near your dwelling; for He shall give His *angels* charge over you."[19] Angels are involved in protecting us from evil and plague. They protect us from accidents, from dashing our foot against a stone. They protect us from plague, stroke, sickness, infectious diseases, and wounds. Though we may experience some of these things, what we go through is far less in frequency and severity due to the presence of the angels. Based on these verses, angels minister in the areas of *protection* and *health*.

The power of one angel

In the days of King Hezekiah, a righteous king, Jerusalem was under siege by Sennacherib, the king of Assyria. King Hezekiah prayed for

---

[14] Acts 5:19–20
[15] Acts 12:7–10
[16] Acts 27:23–24
[17] Revelation 5:11, Hebrews 12:22
[18] Hebrews 1:14
[19] Psalm 91:10

help, and God heard his prayer. In one night, the angel of the Lord went forth and killed one hundred and eighty-five thousand Assyrians.[20] Sennacherib departed and never returned.

One day God will send an angel to bind Satan with a great chain and throw him into the bottomless pit. He doesn't need a legion of angels, just one.[21] Remember, Satan has been stripped of his heavenly powers. He is no match for a holy warring angel, such as Michael, the archangel.

> ***The blood covenant made with Abraham and his seed included the protective, helping ministry of angels— perhaps for the first time in human history!***

Angels listen for God's Word

Bless the LORD, you His angels,
Who excel in strength, who do His word,
Heeding the voice of His word.
> —*Psalm 103:20 (italics added)*

Angels listen for God's Word and do it. If you make the Word of God part of your everyday speech, affirming that you are what God's Word says you are, that you have what God's Word says you have, and that you can do what God's Word says you can do, your angels are *loosed* to bring God's Word to pass. The God who spoke the written Word is still alive. His Words are truth and have never lost their power. Whether spoken by Moses, the Prophets, Jesus, the apostles, or you today (with a right heart), the Word of God has authority, and the angels recognize it when you speak His Word and in alignment with His Word.

However, if the words you say contradict what God has said, your angels are forced to stand idly by, not hearing anything they can heed and do. How often have we *bound* our heavenly help by the ignorant, unbelieving words of our mouths? Heaven is not moved by the simple

---

[20] 2 Kings 19:35
[21] Revelation 20:1–3

fact of our need—everyone has needs—it is moved by our words of faith.[22] When you declare your faith in God's Word, the angels go to work for you.

The "Double Camp"

So Jacob went on his way, and the angels of God met him. When Jacob saw them, he said, "This is God's camp." And he called the name of that place *Mahanaim*.

—Genesis 32:1–2 (italics added)

The angel of the LORD encamps all around those who fear
    Him,
And delivers them.

—Psalm 34:7

Jacob, as an heir of the promises of God, walked under the shield of divine protection. Where he camped, the angels camped. The meaning of *Mahanaim* (above) is "Double Camp." If you are a born-again Christian, where you live is *Mahanaim*. Though your eyes may not see them, the angels assigned to you and your family camp all around you. Have you ever heard the surround sound demo in a movie theater? A voice says, "It's all around you." That's the way the angels are.

Elisha the prophet had a young servant who was not aware of the "double camp." One night the army of the king of Syria surrounded the tiny village where Elisha lived. In the morning when the young man went outside, he saw Syrian forces encircling the village and ran inside to tell Elisha. The young man was confused by the calm faith of the prophet despite the clear and present danger. Elisha prayed the Lord would open his eyes and show him the *angelic* forces.

So he answered, "Do not fear, for those who are with us are more than those who are with them." And Elisha prayed, and said, "LORD, I pray, open his eyes that he may see." Then the LORD opened the eyes of the young man, and he saw. And behold, the mountain was full of horses and chariots of fire all around Elisha.

—2 Kings 6:16–17

---

[22] Mark 11:22–24

Guardian angels

The Bible does not tell us specifically whether we have guardian angels assigned to us, but we know a few things. God created an innumerable company of angels, more than enough to guard several billion people. The Bible records the presence of angels at Jesus' birth and resurrection. Jesus spoke of the angels who carried the beggar Lazarus at his death to Abraham's bosom.[23] If angels are present at the beginning of life and the end of life and intervene in crises, we can reasonably assume angels guard and protect God's covenant people.

Jesus spoke of the angels assigned to children in Israel, the only nation at that time in covenant with God. The Jews did two things to bring their children under the covenant of protection. They circumcised male sons[24] and dedicated them to the Lord in the temple. Jesus spoke the following of Jewish children who were circumcised and presented.

> "Take heed that you do not despise one of these little ones [children], for I say to you that in heaven their angels always see the face of My Father who is in heaven."
>
> —*Matthew 18:10*

Here is what Mary and Joseph did for Jesus when He was a baby.

> And when eight days were completed for *the circumcision of the Child,* His name was called JESUS, the name given by the angel before He was conceived in the womb. Now when the days of her purification according to the law of Moses were completed, *they brought Him to Jerusalem to present Him to the Lord* (as it is written in the law of the Lord, "Every male who opens the womb shall be called holy to the LORD"), and to offer a sacrifice according to what is said in the law of the Lord, "A pair of turtledoves or two young pigeons."
>
> —*Luke 2:21–24 (italics added)*

It makes sense that when believing parents present or dedicate children to the Lord in Jesus' name, or circumcise them into the covenant of

---

[23] Luke 16:22
[24] Genesis 17:10–14

Abraham, that angels are authorized to do more for them than if they had not been circumcised or dedicated. Otherwise, why would the Bible instruct us to do such things? God established no empty rituals.

The role of angels in protection

So how does God protect us now that we are people of covenant and praying in the name of Jesus? The angels of God camp around believers. Every believer's home is *Mahanaim,* a double camp. When a person with evil intent comes against a person under covenant protection, God will counsel them not to do evil. But if they persist in coming to the double camp, the angels take measures to protect and defend those under protection. At this point, having entered the holy presence of the camp, the would-be perpetrator usually softens and changes their behavior. But I have heard eyewitness accounts of protective miracles done for believers in danger, including handguns that jammed and didn't fire and well-aimed shots that went wide or low.

The prophet Elisha (just mentioned) was surrounded by the Syrian army, but the angelic army of horses and chariots of fire blinded the Syrians' eyes and took them captive without firing a shot. With God's help, Jesus escaped one angry mob intent on throwing Him over a cliff and another that wanted to stone Him. Angelic protection is real.

Ministering spirits

Are they [the angels] not all ministering spirits sent forth to minister for those who will inherit salvation [us]?

—*Hebrews 1:14*

Angels minister on behalf of the heirs of salvation, keeping them safe from physical injury and the forces of darkness. While much of what angels do happens out of our sight, *we* have an active role to play in the effectiveness of their ministry. Our part is to pray daily for safety, believe we are protected, walk in wisdom, and confess that God has given His angels charge over us to keep us everywhere we go.

Angels are bound by our choices

However, if we choose to open a door to the devil, our angels have to stand aside. Like Adam, we can give the devil entrance. The enemy has a legal right to traffic in the darkness we allow. But as soon as we "wake up" and repent, closing those doors and trusting Christ to help us, our angels will fight again to defend our righteous choices.

We are not to worship angels

We are not to worship angels or pray to angels. When the apostle John fell at the feet of an angel to worship him, the angel stopped him and told him, "Worship God!"[25]

Angels help at the moment of death

Angels also help us at the moment of death and escort us into the presence of the Lord as they did for the beggar who died. Good advice for dying people is this: stay in your body until you see the holy angel, and then take his hand and don't let go. Of course, Jesus Himself promised to come for believers. Either way He has you covered.

> "And if I go and prepare a place for you, I will come again and receive you to Myself; that where I am, there you may be also."
> —*John 14:3*

> "So it was that the beggar died, and was carried by the angels to Abraham's bosom. The rich man also died and was buried."
> —*Luke 16:22*

I thank You, Father, that I am in covenant with You through Jesus Christ. Thank You for the angels encamped around me and my family, protecting us from harm. I dwell in the secret place of the Most High, and no evil will befall me nor shall any plague come near my dwelling. I invite and receive the blessing of Your angels now, in Jesus' name.

---

[25] Revelation 19:10

Taking an active role in our own protection

Since we are members of God's covenant, holy angels minister to us, and that's one of the benefits of living in the light. Though some angels have fallen, and we'll talk about them next, the protection that God provides is far more powerful.

SECRET #5: Powerful angels camp around you. They protect, help, and deliver you in ways you can't always see. God's angels guard you day and night, and you release them to do their jobs when you confess Jesus as Lord, pray, and speak faith-filled words.

CHAPTER SIX

Standing Taller than Fallen Angels

The devil, who deceived them, was cast into the lake of fire and brimstone where the beast and the false prophet are. And they will be tormented day and night forever and ever. —Revelation 20:10

Were you ever around a bully in school? Then you'll understand this chapter. The devil is nothing more than a grade-school bully who shouldn't get more credit than he deserves. This chapter helps you understand the greatness of God and the limitations of spiritual darkness. If you've ever lit a match in a dark room or turned on a tiny flashlight, you know that any source of light sends darkness scurrying. Darkness can never overcome the light.

The devil is nothing more than a fallen angel—a created being who rebelled against his Maker.[1] While Eastern religions picture good and evil as equal but opposite, God and the devil are opposite but in no way equal.[2] God created all things, and it's impossible for a fallen angel to be in the same league with the One who made him.

---

[1]   Ezekiel 28:13

[2]   God is good. Good existed first. Evil is a corruption of good. In God, evil is absent. In hell, good is absent. Hell is a corrupt place, far worse than earth, devoid of love, grace, mercy, light, life, and truth, which come from God. Hell was made for the devil and his angels, not for men. Don't think for an instant hell might be tolerable.

The devil fell from heaven

Once intelligent, talented, and beautiful, the devil wouldn't admit that his gifts came from God. Pride overtook him, he thought he was as good as God, and he rebelled. So the Lord stripped him of his heavenly gifts (the good) and booted him out of the third heaven to the second heaven,[3] where the Bible now calls him the "prince of the power of the air."[4] A cut-off branch withers, shrivels, and loses its vitality. It never gains power.

To get back at God (whom he can't attack directly), he tries to corrupt the human race, which God loves. He is like a madman on a mission to destroy a famous painting. Man is the highest creation of God, His classic artistic work, and the enemy attempts to destroy mankind from within. He operates in the second heaven, influencing men through lies, deception, pride, anger, and fear.

His followers were kicked out with him

One third of the angels followed the devil in his rebellion. God also kicked them out of the third heaven[5] to the second heaven and removed His love, light, and truth. These fallen angels became what we call demons. Once instruments of blessing, they are now deceptive, evil, heartless and cruel, afflicting mankind with problems and infirmities. Jesus had power over demons and cast them out to free people from the afflictions they caused.

The devil and his demons are instigators of the war, poverty, and death often blamed on God. Being spirits without bodies, they are powerless to do anything unless they find a human being to do their bidding. They tempt humanity with things that destroy trust in society, such as disrespect, murder, adultery, stealing, lying, and false accusation. They promote false religions and occultic practices that confuse belief in the one true God. Demons contribute to pain, disease, and

---

[3] The devil's fall from the third heaven was recorded in Isaiah 14:12–15, where he is called Lucifer. One day God will send a holy angel to bind him and cast him into the bottomless pit. His ultimate destination will be the lake of fire. Revelation 20:1–3, 10.

[4] Ephesians 2:2

[5] Revelation 12:4, 2 Peter 2:4, Jude :6

accidents. Demons enslave some through addictions to drugs, alcohol, tobacco, pornography, and sexual uncleanness. They incite others to attack women and children and lurk behind child abuse, sexual abuse, rape, spousal abuse, verbal abuse, name-calling, covetousness, greed, and bullying. They stir up envy, strife, and violence.

One of the devil's greatest strategies is magnifying differences between groups, such as men and women, labor and management, those with differing skin colors, people from different cultures, liberals and conservatives, and rich and poor. Jesus warned clearly that kingdoms divided against themselves are headed for destruction and will not be able to stand.[6]

Many blame God for the havoc demons cause, but Jesus attributed stealing, killing, and destroying to the thief, the devil. He taught us to discern between the works of the thief and the work of the Lord,[7] as we'll see in the chapter, "Is It God or the Devil?"

Jesus and you are more powerful than the devil

Jesus demonstrated power over the devil, and the Spirit of Jesus lives in you. You have authority over demons in Jesus' name.

> "Let me illustrate this further. Who is powerful enough to enter the house of a strong man like Satan and plunder his goods? Only someone even stronger—someone who could tie him up and then plunder his house."
>
> —*Mark 3:27 (NLT)*

> In this way, He [Jesus] disarmed the spiritual rulers and authorities. He shamed them publicly by his victory over them on the cross.
>
> —*Colossians 2:15 (NLT)*

> You are of God, little children, and have overcome them, because He who is in you is greater than he who is in the world.
>
> —*1 John 4:4*

---

6   Matthew 12:25
7   John 10:10

See the devil like Jesus and the apostles did

Jesus, the apostles, and the great men and women of God (part of the great cloud of witnesses[8]) were not afraid of the devil. They understood he was a defeated foe. Here's one example.

One night, evangelist Smith Wigglesworth woke from sleep, sensing an evil presence. As he prayed and looked around his bedroom, he saw the devil standing in the corner. "Oh, it's only you," he said as he rolled over and went back to sleep. When we realize who we are in Christ, we will not be intimidated.

The devil is a liar and the inventor of lies

When I meet someone for the first time, I wonder if they are trustworthy? Can I believe what they say? When it comes to the devil, he is a documented liar who hates the truth. The tools of his trade are lies, so he cannot be trusted. Jesus described him like this:

> "… He was a *murderer* from the beginning. He has always hated the truth, because there is no truth in him. When he *lies*, it is consistent with his character; *for he is a liar and the father of lies.*"
>
> —*John 8:44 NLT (italics added)*

The enemy is a deceiver

The devil's greatest weapon is deception, fueled by lies and half-truths. Jesus warned that when He went back to heaven deceivers would come, walking in the spirit of the enemy. He said false prophets and false Christ's will deceive, if possible, even the elect.[9] Scripture reveals that the devil will deceive nations in the end time.[10]

Knowing the truth is the best protection against lying deception. What is truth? God's Word is truth,[11] and the Spirit of truth[12] lives in us, so we do not have to fear.

---

[8] Hebrews 12:1
[9] Matthew 24:4, 5, 11, 24
[10] Revelation 12:9, 13:14, 20:3, 8, 10
[11] John 17:17, 2 Thessalonians 2:9–13
[12] John 14:16, 15:26, 16:13

I once heard Reinhard Bonnke, the late evangelist to Africa, tell this story. A man was startled out of a sound sleep by a loud, intimidating roar. It sounded like a lion was in his bedroom, and he began to tremble with fear. The next roar was even louder, and he shook violently. As he switched on the light, he expected to see a lion ready to pounce, but he couldn't see anything. That's when he noticed in the corner a mouse with a megaphone, roaring like a lion.

The devil goes about *like* a roaring lion, but he isn't one. The Lion of the tribe of Judah has defeated him. As children of God, we need to be aware of the devil's devices but we need not fear him. The day will come when all will see him for who he is, a small and despicable creature. We will be surprised that he could cause such a commotion on earth.

> "Those who see you will gaze at you,
> And consider you, saying:
> 'Is this the man who made the earth tremble,
> Who shook kingdoms,
> Who made the world as a wilderness
> And destroyed its cities,
> Who did not open the house of his prisoners?'"
> —Isaiah 14:16–17 (compare vv. 12–15)

The devil's power is limited

It doesn't take a lot of wisdom to realize God is more powerful than the devil. We know God is *omnipotent* (all-powerful), *omniscient* (all-knowing), and *omnipresent* (everywhere present). The devil lacks these attributes. If he had the power to destroy Christians and the nation of Israel, he would have done so long before now. Demons' knowledge is also limited. They cannot read God's mind or yours. (What they know comes from what you tell them. So, guard your tongue and give them no sign that what they are doing affects you.) Lastly, the devil is limited to one place at a time. He spends his time with world leaders, not in your bedroom. He assigns other demons to do his local dirty work.

Demons do not die

Demon spirits do not die like people but live on in the second heaven. They work through family bloodlines and help the sins of the forefathers pass from generation to generation. Don't give them permission to enter and control your life. That person taking his first drink never planned to be an alcoholic; he simply wanted to have fun with his friends. He did not realize that unseen forces could use alcohol to destroy his life and that of family members yet unborn. God prepared hell as a place for the devil and demons in order to keep them away from His children.[13]

The devil has no more access to God's presence

When the enemy fell from heaven the first time, God apparently allowed him access to the heavenly court, as recorded in Job 1 and 2 and Zechariah 3:1–2. But when Satan caused Jesus to be crucified, he was judged, and his access to the third heaven was terminated.[14]

> She [Israel] bore a male Child [Jesus] who was to rule all nations with a rod of iron. And her Child was caught up to God and His throne [after His resurrection]. ... And war broke out in heaven: Michael and his angels fought with the dragon; and the dragon and his angels fought, but they did not prevail, *nor was a place found for them in heaven any longer*. So the great dragon was cast out, that serpent of old, called the Devil and Satan, who deceives the whole world; he was cast to the earth, and his angels were cast out with him. Then I heard a loud voice saying in heaven, "Now salvation, and strength, and the kingdom of our God, and the power of His Christ have come, *for the accuser of our brethren, who accused them before our God day and night, has been cast down.* And they overcame him by the blood of the Lamb and by the word of their testimony, and they did not love their lives to the death.
> —*Revelation 12:5, 6–11 (italics added)*

The events of Job 1 and 2 and Zechariah 3:1–2 can't happen anymore! When God expelled the devil and his angels permanently, no place remained for them in (the third) heaven. Today, God refuses to allow demons in His presence. *He has no conversations with the devil about you and does not sign permission slips for him to attack you!*

The devil can no longer accuse God's people before Him because the "accuser of our brethren... has been cast down." In other words, the

---

[13] Matthew 25:41
[14] John 12:31, Colossians 2:15

devil in his role as prosecuting attorney has been held in contempt and ejected from the courtroom. Only our Defense Attorney, Jesus Christ, is allowed there. (It doesn't hurt that the Judge is our Father.) Believers have overcome the enemy by the blood of the Lamb and the word of their testimony.[15]

The devil is organized

As an evangelist, Paul traveled from city to city preaching the gospel. He often experienced persecution when he went to new territories. After years of trials, Paul discerned the root of the problem.

> We do not wrestle against flesh and blood [human beings], but against principalities, against powers, against the rulers of the darkness of this age, against spiritual hosts of wickedness in the heavenly places.
>
> —*Ephesians 6:12*

Every time Paul went to a new region, the local demonic powers resisted him. The kingdom of darkness is organized. The devil's generals, lieutenants, and privates are assigned territories throughout the world to promote their anti-God, anti-Christ, anti-life agenda.

The point you don't want to miss

Mankind still has free will though evil is present. Principalities and powers rule the world *only when people yield to them.* Though Adam and Eve gave in to the devil, their action did not negate God's sovereign Word granting men dominion and free will. People may yield to deception and evil, but they still have the freedom to choose. Leaders and those in authority over peoples and nations face the strongest battles and need all the prayer they can get. So, while unseen forces try to rule the world, the final decisions rest with people. The devil cannot *force* you to do anything—you still have a choice.

---

[15] Revelation 12:10–11

Principalities

Principalities are the dark princes over nations and regions. They try to manipulate the highest levels of governments because governments have the most power over people. The holy angel sent to Daniel wrestled with the "prince of Persia,"[16] a demonic spirit being over Persia who opposed God's will for Israel. This same principality is still there in the second heaven over Iran (Persia), so don't be surprised when people today do what their ancestors did. Only Christ can set men free of their control.

Powers

Powers are one level down from principalities. These "authorities" have received delegated power from the principality. They try to control influential parts of society like political parties, legislative bodies, regulatory agencies, the justice system, news reporting, and education. As our nation has become increasingly secular with not as many Christians in government, fewer in key positions have the integrity to resist these spirits and promote the general good in a nonpartisan manner. Powers engage on state and local levels too. For example, they attempt to dominate the educational system to turn the young away from God and His principles.

Rulers of the darkness of this age

The phrase "rulers of the darkness of this age" refers to "world-rulers" who are not necessarily government leaders. This broad category includes false religions that cross international boundaries, holding hundreds of millions of people in spiritual and moral darkness. Demons at this level seek to control world-wide cartels such as oil and diamonds, international banking, business and manufacturing empires, the media, and anything possessing *global* impact and power. Hollywood, sports, the music industry, the TV industry, and the video game business have world-wide influence, and demons target them for control. As a result, a lot of darkness is produced and distributed.

---

[16] Daniel 10:13, 20–21

Government, education, media, arts, and entertainment are tools of influence spreading either darkness or light. Any medium that influences the masses attracts the powers of darkness. Good or bad is not in the medium but in the message sent. Godly values build unity and trust, but self-serving values fragment the culture into a million special interest groups, tearing national unity apart. Jesus said, "Every kingdom divided against itself is brought to desolation, and every city or house divided against itself will not stand."[17] Division weakens us from within.

Spiritual hosts of wickedness

Spiritual hosts of wickedness are the lowest order. Multitudes of low-level devils wrestle with us to stir fear, anger, pride, lust, strange thoughts, and compulsive habits. Our job is to overcome these, so the Lord can use us where we live.

> ### The devil cannot force you to do anything—
> ### you still have a choice.

To know what you are up against in your community, identify the opposition to Christianity and godly values. Local government officials? A newspaper? School boards? Activists? We don't wrestle against people but against the spiritual forces behind the people. Every region has distinct issues in the second heaven, some traceable to the area's history. We overcome them by putting on the full armor of God, praying in unity with others, and taking positive action to change things. There is safety, power, and wisdom in numbers, and we need more Christians in public office who are able to withstand ungodly influences. Moses recommended able leaders, who feared God, spoke truth, and hated covetousness (wouldn't take bribes from special interests).[18]

You may sense spiritual warfare as you move to higher levels of influence for Christ. Resistance tests your love and devotion to the Lord. Don't back down or quit because of the pressure. Don't be pushed

---

[17] Matthew 12:25
[18] Exodus 18:21

around by a bully you cannot see. Bring your issue to God. Perhaps you need prayer warriors undergirding your efforts. Intercessory prayer is the engine room of the local church and every effective ministry. Every pastor and church need Spirit-filled intercessors who pray with power and authority.

We must respond to God's call despite the pressures. If Jesus had quit His ministry because of the warfare, we would be lost. When God calls you to go forward, take heart—you'll be helping enough people to justify the battle.

Don't view demonic resistance as a sign you are doing something wrong and then give up. Spiritual warfare is a back-handed compliment that you are a threat to the devil and his agenda. He does not want you standing for God and spreading the word of his defeat. Pressing through resistance testifies that you love the Lord, who promised that "nothing shall by any means hurt you."[19] "For God has not given us a spirit of fear, but of power and of love and of a sound mind."[20] You are of God and have overcome these things "because He who is in you is greater than he who is in the world."[21]

God equips you for ministry even if He needs to send more angels so you cannot be stopped. Set your will to go forward in faith and fulfill your assignment. You and God are the majority.

> "No weapon formed against you shall prosper,
>   And every tongue which rises against you in judgment
>   You shall condemn.
>   This is the heritage of the servants of the LORD,
>   And their righteousness is from Me,"
>   Says the LORD.
>
> —*Isaiah 54:17*

The power of God in the second heaven

God did not give the second heaven over to demons. The Father, Son, Holy Spirit, and holy angels surround and protect believers. Jesus

---

[19] Luke 10:19

[20] 2 Timothy 1:7

[21] 1 John 4:4

Himself promised to be with us always and reveal Himself to us. Though He sat down at God's right hand after His resurrection, Jesus is not confined there. He who planted the vineyard still strolls through it in the spirit. The book of Revelation describes Jesus as a good, diligent, visiting Bishop or Overseer, walking "in the midst" of His churches.[22]

Years after His ascension, Jesus appeared five times to Paul: on the Damascus road, in Corinth, twice in Jerusalem, and in Rome.[23] John saw Him on the Isle of Patmos.[24] These post-ascension visits were not His second coming but the keeping of His promise not to leave us orphans, but to be with us and show Himself to us.[25] He will come again when every eye shall see Him.[26] In the meantime, He visits His Church to direct, encourage, and strengthen us, just as He said. Do you know when Jesus steps into your church? Keep your spiritual eyes open for Him when you celebrate the Lord's Supper.[27]

We have another Helper who dwells in us forever, the Holy Spirit. He teaches us all things and guides us into all truth. Do you have questions about how to do something? Ask the Holy Spirit to help you. Not sure what is true? Ask the Spirit of Truth to reveal to you the truth about anything, even the deep things of God. He communicates God's love, comfort, care, and concern, reminds us of His Word, inspires us to do the right thing, and helps us bring forth the fruit of the Spirit.

Every believer has angels protecting him or her. Holy angels are stronger than demons. (When it's time to bind the devil at the end of Revelation, God sends *one* holy angel, not a legion of them.[28] The devil lost power when he fell.) Angels are free to operate in our lives when we confess Jesus as Lord, confess our faith in Him, and practice what He said.

Aren't you glad you read through this chapter? The God we serve is unlimited, but the enemy we face is limited in power and scope. God operates in love, but the enemy in hate. God lives in the light, but the

---

[22] Revelation 2:1, 1:20

[23] Acts 9:4–6, 18:9–10, 22:17–21, 23:11, 2 Timothy 4:17

[24] Revelation 1:10–18

[25] Matthew 28:20, 18:20, 1:23, John 14:18, 21, 23

[26] Revelation 1:7

[27] Luke 24:30–31

[28] Revelation 20:1–3

enemy in thick darkness. Just one ray of light from the Savior's face dispels the darkness of generations. We are so blessed to be following Jesus.

The next chapters deal with the necessity of prayer, the benefits of faith, pleading the blood, being guided by the Holy Spirit, and dwelling in the secret place of the Most High. You don't want to miss them.

> *Heavenly Father, thank you for revealing that Your power is so much greater than any opposing force. Thank you for being with us always and protecting us, in Jesus' name. Amen.*

SECRET #6: The devil is a fallen angel and not in the God class. Unlike God, he is in one place at a time, lost power when he was thrown out of God's presence, and doesn't know God's plans. The Lord and His angels protect believers and fight for them in the second heaven.

CHAPTER SEVEN

Why You Must Pray

*"Ask, and it will be given to you; seek, and you will find; knock, and
it will be opened to you. For everyone who asks receives, and he who
seeks finds, and to him who knocks it will be opened."*
—*Matthew 7:7–8*

It was dusk on the outskirts of a small town in Colorado as a young
man walked down the center of a road. There was no traffic. Out of
nowhere a voice said, "Get off the road!" He turned to see who spoke,
but no one was there. It was strange. As he continued, he heard the voice
say with authority a second time, "Get off the road!" Puzzled, he stepped
to the shoulder of the road, and a car with its headlights off whizzed
past. He shared this story with me on the way to work one day and asked
what it meant. I said, "The Lord saved your life because He has a purpose for you."

God loves all people and extends grace and protection to them
before they know Him like He did for this young man. Of course, I don't
know how many prayers had been offered on his behalf by a praying
grandmother, parent, neighbor, or friend, but I know someone had been
praying for him. The Lord protected me more than once before I
accepted Christ, and I know now that my relatives were praying for me.
While God can be very gracious to those who don't know Him, His best
blessings come to those who ask. For this reason, prayer is indispensable
to anyone desiring to live in the light of divine protection.

"You do not have because you do not ask..."

The Bible's book of James is known for its plainspoken practicality. James never sugarcoated spiritual truth and made this blunt statement about prayer, *"...you do not have because you do not ask."*[1] Prayer is necessary for God to move on your behalf. After entering the covenant, the first principle of protection is *prayer.* If you want God's help, ask Him! Jesus said, "Ask, and it will be given to you; seek, and you will find; knock, and it will be opened to you."[2] We have not because we ask not.

Personally, for years I acted as though I did not believe that statement. I assumed that God in His sovereign omnipotence took care of everything, whether I prayed or not. Isn't it obvious that an all-powerful God controls all things, so how could my little prayers count for anything? At least, that's how I thought. When we ponder the Lord's greatness and realize He answers to no one, why would He command us to pray?

The answer to this question is simple and profound. As always, we can't seek truth in assumptions—even if we have carried them from childhood. We find truth in God's Word. So take some time and prayerfully read and reread this chapter until it sinks in how important your prayers are.

Free will and the sovereignty of God

In the beginning, it pleased God to make man in His image and give him dominion on earth.

> God said, "Let Us make man in Our image, according to our likeness; *let them have dominion...*"
>
> —*Genesis 1:26 (italics added)*

Dominion in Hebrew means *to rule, dominate, tread down, govern,* and *subdue.* Dominion, the power to rule, included free will, the power to choose. When God gave man free will, He no longer controlled people's choices on earth, and nothing guaranteed that His will would be done.

---

[1] James 4:2d
[2] Matthew 7:7

Think about it. Does God control you or do you control you? Do you always do His will? Probably not in every situation. So if you don't always do the will of God, then God's will is not always being done. If He doesn't control your choices, then He doesn't control everything.

The first couple, Adam and Eve, exercised their free will, ate fruit from the forbidden tree, and empowered the devil on earth. That was not the Lord's will, but He did not intervene to stop them from eating. Why? He had given them the freedom to choose *and* to live with the consequences of their choices.

Neither was it God's will for Cain to kill his brother Abel. But how did the Lord handle this? Did He send an angel to restrain Cain from committing the first murder? No, He *counseled* Cain that evil was at his door (in this case, jealousy and rage), and that he should rule over it. Cain, however, went down in history as the one who committed the first murder because he refused to listen to God (as well as the one who ate the firstfruits of his harvest instead of offering them to the Lord).

Why doesn't the Lord restrain evil when His will isn't being done? For one simple reason: when He put man in charge of earth, He imposed limits on Himself. To interfere with mankind's free will choices would violate His Word. The Lord could have prevented evil by turning man into a robot that always obeyed, but then men would no longer be made in the image of God.

God's Word is as sovereign as He is

Up until the moment God spoke the Word giving man dominion, He could do whatever He wanted. But once He put man in charge, He could not overrule man's choices, or His Word giving man free will would no longer be true. But we know God's Word is true and not a lie[3] and that we are made in the image of God and free to act. We are definitely not soulless robots programmed to always do the will of God.

The Word of God, once spoken, cannot be altered or withdrawn. *God's Word is as sovereign as He is.* Consider these verses:

---

[3]   Titus 1:2

"My covenant I will not break,
Nor alter the word that has gone out of My lips."

—Psalm 89:34 (italics added)

"God is not a man, that He should lie,
Nor a son of man, that He should repent.
Has He said, and will He not do?
Or has He spoken, and will He not make it good?"

—Numbers 23:19 (italics added)

"Heaven and earth will pass away, but My words will by no means pass away."

—Matthew 24:35 (italics added)

> **But when men and women pray—this unique event in which the free will of man and the sovereignty of God come together—amazing things happen!**

For His Word's sake, the Lord cannot give man dominion when He created him and then thousands of years later take back control. As difficult as this may be to understand, God set boundaries on Himself in order to give you and me the freedom to choose and act. The Lord is still sovereign, and He can do anything He wants to do *as long as it does not contradict the Word He has already spoken.*

This is like the king's decree under the law of the Medes and the Persians.[4] In order to set a trap for Daniel, the king's counselors convinced King Darius to make a decree that no one could petition any god or man except the king for thirty days. Despite the decree, Daniel prayed boldly to God every day with his windows open.

When Daniel was accused of illegal prayer, the king tried to undo the law. But he was informed that no law of the Medes and Persians could be changed. So, Daniel was thrown into the lions' den, and God's angel protected him overnight. In the morning, the king was glad Daniel had survived, let him out, and threw Daniel's accusers to the lions.

---

[4] Daniel 6:15

If a man's law could not be altered because it represented the sovereign power of a human kingdom, how much more shall God's decrees not be changed, seeing our sovereign Lord uttered them with all wisdom and foresight.

Here's another example. Suppose you have a boss who announced that you are in charge of a department. But instead of allowing you to develop your skills and learn from your mistakes, he micromanages the department behind your back. Are you in charge like he said? No. His words to you were hollow because he never released control.

The question is: does God micromanage everything on earth, or does man have dominion to rule? Which is it? How do we know? We go to His Word. He said, "Let them have dominion…" So, the evil we see on earth is the result of man's choices, not God's will.

When Jesus went to minister in His home town of Nazareth, He went with the same sovereign power of God that manifested miraculously in other cities, but something strange happened there. His ability to do miracles was limited by human unbelief. Scripture says, "Now He could do no mighty work there, except that He laid His hands on a few sick people and healed them."[5]

No matter how much He longed to, no matter how much divine power flowed through Him in other places, He was not able to do any mighty work there. Why? His townspeople were *offended* at Him. Their offense and lack of faith stopped the sovereign power of God. As a result, they did not see the demonstration of the kingdom of God that was manifested in other places. Their free will choices to be offended limited the power of God.

God's intervention is triggered by your free will

Here's how this applies to prayer. Once God gave man dominion, everything on earth had to be *initiated* by a man or woman. Even redemption had to be accomplished *by One who was fully man* although He was fully God.

As shocking as this may sound, the Lord cannot intervene until a man or woman asks. He does not intervene on the basis of need—we see

---

[5] Mark 6:5 (1–6)

unmet needs everywhere—but only on the basis of prayer and faith. If we wish to see His kingdom come and His will be done, we must partner with Him in prayer. When people overlook this simple truth, they wait for the Lord to *move*...while He waits for them to *pray*. The earth is a mess because of men's prayerlessness, not because God wills it.

Jesus illustrated the triggering effect of a believer's prayers in the following passage:

> "Assuredly, I say to you, whatever *you* bind on earth will be bound in heaven, and whatever *you* loose on earth will be loosed in heaven. Again I say to you that if two of *you* agree on earth concerning anything that they ask, it will be done for them by My Father in heaven."
> —*Matthew 18:18–19 (italics added)*

Prayer activates God's intervention. God doesn't bind or loose until we do. We bind and loose verbally on earth, and God backs us up by binding and loosing in the heavenlies. However, we may be assuming that God takes care of evil spirits for us when we haven't bound them first in prayer. But He can't act until those who have dominion do their job. The fervent prayer of a righteous man or woman, boy or girl, avails much.[6]

My knees shake as I think about how often I don't pray. If I want God's help and intervention for my family and myself, *I* have to initiate it. It won't happen on its own, and I can't trust anyone else to do my praying for me. (Others have their own needs and concerns to pray about.) The responsibility for what happens on earth has been mankind's from the beginning, and you and I must realize our prayers are vital to seeing God move.

Does God want to intervene and help man? Of course, He does. He loves to help. *But the legal requirement rooted in His Word must be fulfilled first*—the ones placed in charge of earth must request His help.

Isn't God "in control"?

But someone will insist, "Well, God is in control." What does that mean? It's easy to *assume* that if an all-powerful God is in control that He must control all things. But there is a big difference between being "in

---

6 James 5:16

control" and controlling everything. Actually, the Bible never says that the Lord is "in control" but rather that the Lord reigns.[7] For example, the king who reigns over a country does not control everything that happens in it, but everyone in the country is accountable to the king for their actions.

As much as I might prefer that God micromanaged all things, He gave me one important responsibility. The Lord only intervenes on what I surrender to Him in prayer. If I desire a smoother path in life, I must pray about everything! If you want to get God involved in your daily life, only you can give Him that invitation through prayer.

Personally, it's taken me a long time to understand this, and here's why. First, I've struggled to believe that God meant it when He said, "Let them have *dominion*..." But that's the Word He spoke, so it must be exactly what He meant. What part of the word dominion don't I understand? Second, this places great responsibility on me. I can no longer blame my circumstances on God's will but must confront my choices, my prayerlessness, and my lack of action.

But still, doesn't it seem preposterous that the great God would put flawed, sinful men and women in charge of anything? However, if you think about it, God is a ruler, and the image in which He made man is that of a ruler who is submitted to and obedient to Him. Maybe you rule only over yourself, your pets, and the bugs that crawl into your house, but you still have dominion under God.

If we've always assumed that God totally dictates everything that happens, our prayer life has probably been respectful but timid and tepid. However, Jesus died to restore us to the original dominion given to man. Once we realize our prayers are *necessary* to trigger God's intervention, they become raw and real. We should look to the Word for the knowledge of God and not to what we assume or what someone told us (no matter how sincere they were).

But don't these ideas make some people think they can order God around? Absolutely not! God still reigns over the universe, is the Judge of all, determines the times and seasons, sovereignly moves men's hearts by inspiring them to do His will, and humbles the proud. We must carry

---

[7] Exodus 15:18, 1 Chronicles 16:31, Psalm 93:1, 96:10, 97:1, 99:1, 146:10

our dominion with humility as the Lord's beloved sons and daughters, answerable to Him. God is all-knowing and all-powerful, but His sovereign Word limits His intervention on earth *until we pray,* because that is the way *He* set things up. He left Himself free to do whatever does not contradict His Word or violate men's free will choices.

For example, people say, "God will send revival when He's ready." But He's been ready for thousands of years and can't do anything until men pray. There have been great revivals in the past, but as Dr. A. T. Pierson observed, "There has never been a spiritual awakening in any country or locality that did not begin in united prayer."[8] Revival was initiated by men inspired by the Holy Spirit, and He responded to their prayers.

Do we want revival? Are we desperate enough to pray it in? God is eager to hear our united prayers and will "do exceedingly abundantly above all that we ask or think."[9]

Won't you take a minute and whisper or raise your voice in prayer to Him whose power and presence permeates creation? Release Him to go to work on your behalf. He waits on you to ask for help, so that He can make all things work together for your good. Prayer works in the home, on the job, and in every area of life.

Don't underestimate your dominion

In Psalm 8, David marveled at the dominion given to man.

> When I consider Your heavens, the work of Your fingers,
> The moon and the stars, which You have ordained,
> What is man that You are mindful of him,
> And the son of man that You visit him?
> For You have made him a little lower than the angels,
> And You have crowned him with glory and honor.
>
> *You have made him to have dominion over the works of Your*
> *   hands;*
> You have put all things under his feet,
> All sheep and oxen—

---

[8] J. Edwin Orr, *Prayer and Revival,*
http://www.revival-library.org/index.php/catalogues-menu/revival-miscellanies/
revival-prayer/prayer-and-revival
[9] Ephesians 3:20

Even the beasts of the field,
The birds of the air,
And the fish of the sea
That pass through the paths of the seas.
O LORD, our Lord,
How excellent is Your name in all the earth!
                           —Psalm 8:3–9 (italics added)

The heaven, even the heavens, are the LORD's;
But the earth He has given to the children of men.
                           —Psalm 115:16 (italics added)

The Lord is not some aloof and uncaring spectator watching earth's drama unfold from a heavenly recliner. No, He longs to help but can't until a man or woman asks. When I was young in Christ and unsure of how things worked, I once read, "When I pray, coincidences happen. When I quit praying, they stop happening." I tested that principle, found it true, and it strengthened my prayer life. Now I continue praying even when it looks like nothing is happening.

Partnering with God

If God had never given man dominion, our prayers would matter little. *But when men and women pray—this unique event in which the free will of man and the sovereignty of God come together—amazing things happen.* If Adam and Eve enabled evil by eating the fruit, how much more do our prayers engage God's love and power. The Father desires to *partner* with His sons and daughters,[10] and this alliance works through prayer. The power is not in you; the power is in your prayer partnership with God. So, if you want the Father's help, do what Jesus taught—ask, seek, and knock![11] God will intervene when we pray as we ought. Archimedes said, "Give me a lever long enough…and I shall move the world." That lever is prayer that engages the awesome power of God.

---

[10] Amos 3:7, John 15:15, Jeremiah 7:25, John 5:19–20

[11] Matthew 7:7–8. Jesus spoke here of three levels of prayer. Asking is a simple request. If there is no answer to the asking prayer, we must seek and keep on seeking, which requires more effort. If the door appears closed and locked, we knock and keep on knocking and must persevere in prayer like the widow coming to the unjust judge, or like Daniel, whose answer was delayed by resistance in the second heaven. Cp Luke 18:1–8, Daniel 10:1–13.

The pattern for our lives was established in the beginning. God walked with Adam in the cool of the day, and they discussed what needed to be done and how to do it. When Adam fell, that communion was broken, but it is restored in Christ. Today, when we choose to walk in the Spirit, the Lord guides our steps by His wisdom and makes our prayers effective by His power.

The example of Jesus

The Spirit-filled Man Christ Jesus modeled the perfect harmony of the free will of man and the sovereign power of God. He spent His early mornings in prayer seeking God's will, and the power of God flowed through Him in miracles and healing.

The will of man and the power of God united again on the Day of Pentecost as the Lord poured out His Spirit. God releases His power through those surrendered to His will. His Spirit guides His sons and daughters in blessing others.

As partners with God, the responsibility for our safety is not God's alone.

To achieve what He did, Jesus prayed daily[12] and taught His disciples to pray daily, "Your kingdom come. Your will be done on earth as it is in heaven."[13] If God's will happened automatically, prayer would be pointless. But Jesus didn't think it was pointless because He set aside time every morning to pray. We, too, must pray or suffer the consequences of prayerlessness—*not* seeing His kingdom come or His will be done. Because of our dominion, the accountability for what happens on earth is ours, not God's.

> *Heavenly Father, forgive my lack of prayer. I commit to pray daily from this point forward. May Your kingdom come and Your will be done in my life and that of my family, in Jesus' name. Amen.*

---

[12] Mark 1:35, Luke 5:16, 6:12, 9:28–29
[13] Matthew 6:10–11

When we pray, we don't have to lower our voice, use big words, and get all religious. Prayer is having a conversation with God in sincere words from the heart. A conversation involves speaking and listening. The Lord knows everything about you, so be honest. Frank talk in the throne room is enlightening as we get things off our chest *and then listen*. Pray at least the Lord's Prayer first thing on arising,[14] not by rote but understanding what the petitions mean. Add your requests.

"In this manner, therefore, pray:

Our Father in heaven,
Hallowed [holy] be Your name.
Your kingdom come.
Your will be done
On earth as it is in heaven.
Give us this day our daily bread.
And forgive us our debts [sins],
As we forgive our debtors [those who sin against us].
And do not lead us into temptation,
But deliver us from the evil one.
For Yours is the kingdom and the power and the glory
    forever. Amen."

—Matthew 6:9–13

Talk to God throughout the day in short, quick, "arrow prayers," which help you abide in His presence. It might be as simple as, "Lord, help me now." "Lord, grant me wisdom on this." Or even Peter's classic prayer when sinking, "Lord, save me!"[15] You may be surprised how much praying you can do at a red light or in a traffic jam.

God seeks prayer warriors

Because prayer is necessary for God to move, He searches for people who pray—for *intercessors*. He needs them.

---

[14] Matthew 6:9–13
[15] Matthew 14:30

"So *I sought for a man* among them who would *make a wall, and stand in the gap* before Me on behalf of the land, that I should not destroy it; but I found no one."

—*Ezekiel 22:30 (italics added)*

So truth fails,
And he who departs from evil makes himself a prey.
Then the LORD saw it, and it displeased Him
That there was no justice.
He saw that there was no man,
And wondered that there was no intercessor;
Therefore His own arm brought salvation for Him;
And His own righteousness, it sustained Him.

—*Isaiah 59:15–16 (italics added)*

"…if My people who are called by My name will humble themselves, and pray and seek My face, and turn from their wicked ways, then I will hear from heaven, and will forgive their sin and heal their land."

—*2 Chronicles 7:14*

God looks for prayer partners to identify the "gap in the wall" and pray for the land so He can help.

God needs people of prayer, but He also needs people of action. Asking for the Lord's help raises up leaders who put feet to prayer and change the course of history. But many recline on their couches, neither praying nor doing, wondering why God doesn't take care of the poverty, war, and violence. At the same time God sits on His throne, wondering why His people do not call on Him to raise up leaders to change things. Have we lulled ourselves to spiritual sleep, thinking God controls all things without us lifting a finger? As Dr. Phil says, "How is that working for you?" You can't just sit—pray or do something!

Put your prayers "on the record"

When you have a need, stop what you are doing and ask the Father in Jesus' name. Put your petition on God's official prayer record. When we get to heaven and ask, "Why did Brother or Sister So-and-So get something and I did not?" God will pull out His logbook of prayer requests, scroll down with His finger, and say, "I can't find the record of you asking for that." Thinking about your need is not enough. "Well, the Lord knows what I need." No, put it into words and make a formal request, whether it's a whisper or a shout. *We have not because we ask not.*

As partners with God, the responsibility for our safety and success is not God's alone. We must pray daily, "And do not lead us into temptation, but deliver us from the evil one."[16] If we don't want temptation or the evil one messing with us or our family, then we must open our mouths and ask God for help. Jesus told us to pray *before* being led into temptation. This is proactive prayer. It's easier to quench a fire when it's small than to put it out when the house is engulfed in flames.

> *Father, in Jesus' name, I ask You to protect me (and my family) from _____. Also, help me (us) with _____. Lead us not into temptation and deliver us from the evil one. Thank You for Your intervening grace, in Jesus' name. Amen.*

And when you are praying, don't pray for your family only, pray for all men.[17] How can God give grace to those who don't know Him, like the young man mentioned at the beginning of this chapter, unless someone lays up prayers God can use? If serious prayer went up in a community for all men, revival would break out.

Thank God for the grace of our Lord Jesus Christ, who intercedes at God's right hand, making up what is lacking in our imperfect prayers. Thank God for the Holy Spirit who inspires us to pray. In the next chapter we'll find out how to add faith to our prayers.

SECRET #7: God's kingdom comes and His will is done only when man prays. To receive divine intervention, you must exercise your free will and ask for God's amazing help in Jesus' name.

---

[16] Matthew 6:13, Psalm 141:9

[17] 1 Timothy 2:1–4

CHAPTER EIGHT

Walk by Faith, Not Sight

So Jesus answered and said to them, "Have faith in God."
—Mark 11:22

King David endured many hard things in his life, but he walked in God's protection as Abraham's descendant. He trusted in God. When things weren't going his way, he drew the Lord to himself by speaking faith-filled words and singing of His presence and protection—even when his outward circumstances were life-threatening. The shield of faith guarded this seasoned warrior through many battles, so we can learn from him—the man after God's own heart. The following Psalms reveal the faith of a king who openly worshiped the Lord.

> I will love You, O LORD, my strength.
> The LORD is my rock and my fortress and my deliverer;
> *My God, my strength, in whom I will trust;*
> *My shield and the horn of my salvation, my stronghold.*
> I will call upon the LORD, who is worthy to be praised;
> So shall I be saved from my enemies.
>
> *—Psalm 18:1–3 (italics added)*

> In God (I will praise His word),
> In the LORD (I will praise His word),
> *In God I have put my trust;*
> I will not be afraid.
> What can man do to me?
>
> *—Psalm 56:10–11 (italics added)*

Be merciful to me, O God, be merciful to me!
For my soul trusts in You;
And in the shadow of Your wings I will make my refuge,
Until these calamities have passed by.

—*Psalm 57:1 (italics added)*

But I will sing of Your power;
Yes, I will sing aloud of Your mercy in the morning;
For You have been my defense
And refuge in the day of my trouble.
To You, O my Strength, I will sing praises;
For God is my defense,
My God of mercy.

—*Psalm 59:16–17 (italics added)*

Hear my cry, O God;
Attend to my prayer.
From the end of the earth I will cry to You,
When my heart is overwhelmed;
Lead me to the rock that is higher than I.
For You have been a shelter for me,
A strong tower from the enemy.
I will abide in Your tabernacle forever;
I will trust in the shelter of Your wings.

Selah
—*Psalm 61:1–4 (italics added)*

When I remember You on my bed,
I meditate on You in the night watches.
Because You have been my help,
Therefore in the shadow of Your wings I will rejoice.

—*Psalm 63:6–7 (italics added)*

Why am I discouraged?
Why is my heart so sad?
I will put my hope in God!
I will praise him again—my Savior and my God!

—*Psalm 42:11 (NLT)*

David called on the Lord as his refuge, strength, defense, shelter, rock, and strong tower. He rejoiced under the shadow of God's wings.

He sang aloud, confessing God's power to defend and protect him. When overwhelmed, David prayed, "Lead me to the rock that is higher than I." Protection comes to people of faith, prayer, and a positive outlook. Believe God is on your side and protects you, and pray daily as Jesus taught.

What is faith?

Faith is key to receiving from God, so what exactly is it? Faith means believing—really believing—that God is real and His Words are true. Abraham's faith is the classic example.

> Then He brought him outside and said, "Look now toward heaven, and count the stars if you are able to number them." And He said to Him, "So shall your descendants be." And he believed in the Lord, and He accounted it to him for righteousness.
>
> —*Genesis 15:5–6*

Abraham's faith wasn't blind, for it was based on the promise the sovereign God made, "So shall your descendants be." It pleased God when Abraham believed His Word, and He counted it as *righteousness*.

The Bible defines faith as "the substance of things hoped for, the evidence of things not seen."[1] Faith is the underlying confidence that things hoped for (but not yet seen) are a reality in the spirit, soon to be manifested in the natural. Faith takes possession of the promise before the answer is seen. Faith is like receiving the deed to a piece of property you've never visited. You *know* it's yours before you ever walk on it. A few verses later the writer of Hebrews states, "But without faith it is impossible to please [God]…"[2] The Lord is pleased when people trust His Word, and He calls them righteous. We can't be pleasing to God if we don't believe His Word, because that is very close to calling Him a liar.

Suppose something you need is stored on a high shelf. If you are not tall enough to reach it on your own, you get a stool. If you trust the stool to carry your weight, you can take hold of the item. If you have the stool but don't trust it, the object remains out of reach.

---

[1] Hebrews 11:1
[2] Hebrews 11:6

Believing God's Word is like standing on a step stool. When we trust it, we obtain promises that are otherwise out of reach. But if we allow fear, doubt, and unbelief to dominate us, we come short of what God planned for us to receive.

How do we increase our faith?

Fortunately, we don't have to let fear and doubt take advantage of our ignorance. Our faith grows and abounds when we hear faith-filled teaching that shows us how to put our trust in God and His Word.

> So then faith comes by hearing, and hearing by the word of God.
> —*Romans 10:17*

Faith comes by hearing. Faith comes when we seriously listen as the Word is preached and taught and when we prayerfully read the Bible for ourselves. Faith comes when the Holy Spirit floods our hearts with understanding and causes the Word to come alive. It comes as the Lord speaks personally[3] to us, His faithful servants.

> *Believing God's Word is like standing on a step stool. When we trust it, we obtain promises that are otherwise out of reach.*

When God's Word enters our heart, we are flooded with the light of His Spirit. That light imparts faith and exposes the devil's lies. When we discern the lies, we replace them with the truth of His Word, and our faith increases.

Faith is a growing thing that takes time to develop. As a new Christian, I struggled to believe because I was ignorant of God's Word and my faith was undeveloped. I hadn't heard much preaching or teaching to increase my faith and had only seen a few prayers answered. Older, mature believers trusted God for what they could not see while I sought to see something to help me believe. I felt like a kid watching basketball players dunk the ball when I struggled to throw it as high as the rim.

---

[3]   John 10:27

Now I can trust without seeing first, but developing my faith took time. To make it grow, I had to become a "Word person." That's someone who believes that the Bible is God speaking to them personally. I read the Word to find out what it said and did my best to apply it to my life. I also became a "church person," being at church every time the doors were open, so I could learn and absorb everything I could about God and His Word.

The two components of faith

Faith has two components that reinforce each other: (1) *Faith in the character of God.* Are you convinced of His steadfast love, faithful care, and watchful provision? (2) *Faith in His recorded promises.* Do you believe the wonderful promises God made to you in Christ, that are Yes and Amen?[4] The two components are inseparable. The promises originated in God's character, in His heart of love, care, and compassion. Moreover, His faithful lovingkindness causes His Word to come to pass. So, if you are focused on His person, remember the promises came from Him, too. If you are looking more at the promises, remember the great love of Him who made them and His faithfulness in keeping them.

Prayer and faith work hand in hand. You pray because you believe. You obey because you believe. Your words and works reveal your faith. If you are struggling to believe, go where the Word is preached and taught. Set aside a daily time to read the Bible. Pray for wisdom and understanding. Your faith will grow abundantly, and you'll end up living in the light instead of in the darkness of lies, deception, and unbelief.

Next, we'll turn to using the powerful weapon of the blood of Jesus.

Heavenly Father, as I now meditate in Your Word, increase my faith. Help me encourage myself in the Lord as I trust Your character, promises, and faithfulness. As You blessed David for His faith, bless my prayers for my family and myself, in Jesus' Name. Amen.

SECRET #8: Once you have prayed, you must stand strong in faith and patience, trusting God's revealed Word and His faithful lovingkindness to bring His Word to pass.

---

4 2 Corinthians 1:20

CHAPTER NINE

What Does It Mean to Plead the Blood?

*But if we walk in the light as He is in the light, we have fellowship
with one another, and the blood of Jesus Christ His Son cleanses us
from all sin. —1 John 1:7*

A s a new Christian, feeling forgiven and accepted by God was the
most important thing to me. In those days guilt tracked me like a
hound dog on a scent, and I had a hard time blocking the memory of
past mistakes. I was born again, baptized in water and in the Holy Spirit,
but for seven years I struggled with not feeling accepted by God—until I
heard a skilled preacher tell this story about the blood of Christ.

A man had a teenage son who had just learned to drive. He was a
good kid, and his father loved him. The son asked if he could take the
car on Friday night to go out with friends. The father agreed after telling
him when to come home. That night as the father went to bed, he
couldn't sleep. When his son failed to return on time, he began to pray.
That's when he got the phone call no parent wants to receive. "Do you
have a son by this name? There's been an accident, and you need to
come now."

The father jumped in his car and sped to the crash site. As he got out
of the car, he saw his son lying on the side of the road, seriously injured.
An ambulance had arrived, and the paramedic said, "Is this your son?
He needs blood, and we don't have his type." The father said, "My son

and I have the same blood type. You can give him my blood." The man said, "Okay, but this is going to hurt." The father said, "I'll do whatever it takes. Just save his life."

The paramedic had the man lie beside his son. He inserted a tube into a vein in the man's arm and connected it to one in the boy's arm. Then he told the man, "Pump!" The father clenched his fist and squeezed his muscles rhythmically to force blood into his son's body. The paramedic became emotional as he watched the father giving life to his son and broke the rules by asking, "How does it feel, man? How does it feel?" The father answered, "It feels like the pains of hell, but he's my son! He's my son!"

This illustration of God's love moved me to tears as I realized my heavenly Father's love for me was far greater than my mistakes. For years I had judged myself unworthy of the love of God, and it was time to forgive myself and accept the life-giving power of the blood. We each have our struggles in the Christian life, and this was mine—God had forgiven me, but I hadn't been able to forgive myself.

Receiving Christ as Savior starts a life-saving transfusion, and the blood of Christ revives us after the wreck we've made of our lives. It brings us into the Father's presence where we are forgiven, cleansed, and accepted as though we had never sinned. "There is therefore now *no condemnation* for those who are in Christ Jesus."[1]

The benefits of the blood

In Bible days, men sacrificed animals to atone for sin, and their blood was sprinkled on the altar. Those sacrifices pointed to the coming of the Lamb of God. When John the Baptist perceived that Jesus was the Messiah, He proclaimed, "Behold the Lamb of God who takes away the sin of the world!"[2] As the son of a temple priest, John presented Jesus to the world as the ultimate sacrificial offering.

Ephesians declares that Jesus' blood provided *redemption* and abundant *forgiveness.*

---

[1] Romans 8:1 (ESV)
[2] John 1:29

In Him we have *redemption* through His blood, the *forgiveness* of sins, according to the riches of His grace.

—*Ephesians 1:7 (italics added)*

Colossians states we are *reconciled* to God by the blood.

And by Him [Christ] to *reconcile* all things to Himself, by Him, whether things on earth or things in heaven, having made peace through the blood of His cross.

—*Colossians 1:20 (italics added)*

Romans teaches we are *justified* by the blood—declared righteous in God's eyes.

Much more then, having now been *justified* by His blood, we shall be saved from wrath through Him.

—*Romans 5:9 (italics added)*

Jesus declared that His blood sealed a *new covenant* between God and all believers.

"For this is *My blood of the new covenant,* which is shed for many for the remission of sins."

—*Matthew 26:28 (italics added)*

The blood provides forgiveness and right standing with God, making us heirs of God's best blessings. Jesus bore in His body every bit of punishment for sin the Father required. His blood redeems us out from under the devil's authority, removing his right to oppress us. Christ's blood reconciles us to the Father, so that He counts us as His own sons and daughters, members of the family He cherishes and protects. The blood of Christ seals our covenant with God, so He never leaves us nor forsakes us, nor can anyone pluck us out of His hands.

And we don't have to be perfect to receive these life-changing benefits, only to believe in the power of Christ's shed blood.

"Pleading the blood"

But many saints use the blood in an additional way, "pleading the blood" for protection. I had to ask what it meant the first few times I heard the term. Some visualized being encircled with a "bloodline" the enemy could not cross, but I was confused because I didn't know where this was in the Bible. We'll talk more about that in a moment.

One day I discovered the meaning of the word "pleading," and my understanding grew by leaps and bounds. In today's English, pleading refers to an earnest entreaty, a persuasive argument, and sometimes begging. But it's an old legal term that originally meant *to plead, to enter a plea,* or *to argue a case in a court of law.* It slowly dawned on me that "pleading the blood" is the legal proceeding at the heart of all intercessory prayer.

Pleading the blood means…presenting the blood of Jesus to God the Judge as evidence for acquittal on all charges.

God the Father sits as Judge over the heavenly Supreme Court. Before Him is the Mercy Seat sprinkled with the blood of Jesus. Pleading the blood means arguing a case before God by presenting the blood of Christ as *evidence* for acquittal on all charges.

Because the blood of Christ is continually present on the Mercy Seat as proof that Jesus bore the penalty of sin, the Father raps His gavel and forgives the one who has come to faith in Christ. Punishment no longer applies. The blood testifies that Jesus bore sin's penalty in their place and speaks of His atoning, sacrificial *death.*

But Christ's blood also contains the divine, innocent *life* that is sprinkled on believers at the moment of forgiveness. Sprinkling illustrates a transfer. The life imparted by the blood of Christ is powerful, so powerful that when it touches a spiritually-dead human heart, it re-creates it, makes it new, and causes it to partake of the divine nature.[3]

Forgiveness alone (based on Christ's *death*) does not make a full atonement, because man needs a change of nature to stop sinning. The *divine life* in the blood of Jesus, which is infused with His sinless Spirit, regenerates hearts and gives believers the power to overcome sin.

---

[3] Hebrews 10:22, 12:24, Ezekiel 36:26–27, 2 Peter 1:4, 2 Corinthians 5:17, Titus 3:5

The blood on the Mercy Seat thus provides two things: (1) *forgive-ness of sins,* and (2) a *changed nature,* the power to go and sin no more. Jesus illustrated how grace works when the Pharisees brought Him a woman caught in adultery. When her accusers had left, He said to her, "Neither do I condemn you; go and sin no more."[4] In the act of forgiving her, He empowered her to go and sin no more. What grace this is! By the death of Christ, righteousness is *imputed* to us, and we are forgiven. By the life in His blood, righteousness is *imparted* to us, and we are empowered to sin no more.

The writer of Hebrews went on to say that blood "speaks."[5] The blood of Abel cried for justice, but the blood of Christ spoke better things: "Father, forgive them for they do not know what they do. Father, fill them with My life and Spirit, so they may go and sin no more."

> " 'For the *life* of the flesh is *in the blood,* and I have given it to you upon the altar to make atonement for your souls; for it is the blood that makes atonement for the soul.' "
>
> —*Leviticus 17:11 (italics added)*

> *And they overcame him* [the adversary] *by the blood of the Lamb* and by the word of their testimony, and they did not love their lives to the death.
>
> —*Revelation 12:11 (italics added)*

Pleading the blood is true intercession

Pleading the blood is the highest form of priestly intercession. As we stand before the Judge for another, we present two facts: (1) Jesus bore the penalty of sins; (2) Jesus' righteous life and Spirit (permeating His blood) can be transferred to the one for whom we pray. His sin-conquering, death-defeating, triumphant Spirit of life has the power to cleanse and transform any man or woman, boy or girl. Pleading the case based on the merits of the blood prepares the way for forgiveness and a new nature, a new heart, and a new beginning. The Holy Spirit delivers the life in the blood of Jesus to the person for whom we pray in order to lead them to

---

4   John 8:11
5   Hebrews 12:24

repentance, cleansing, and to overcome sin. The apostle John taught that God gives *life* to those for whom we pray.[6]

Intercession can never override others' free will choices nor can it save those who have not yet received Christ, but it releases the Holy Spirit to draw them to Jesus. The Lord stores up our prayers until the person for whom we pray turns to Him. Then He answers mightily.

Pleading the blood is the most powerful prayer you can offer. *Pray with full authority as a priest standing before God.* You can do this during the Lord's Supper with the elements representing His body and blood, or imagine yourself kneeling before the heavenly Mercy Seat. Don't be intimidated by this thought because God called us a "kingdom of priests."[7] The way into the heavenly Holy of Holies is open now,[8] and we are to come boldly because the Spirit of Jesus, our High Priest, lives big within us. When we intercede, the Holy Spirit guides us how to pray.

> *Heavenly Father, I come now before the Mercy Seat in intercession for _____ , presenting the blood of Jesus, the Lamb of God. Christ's blood declares that a death occurred, bearing the just penalty of sin. Judicially, I transfer the sins of _____ to Christ. I pray their sins be forgiven because the price has been paid. I ask that the righteousness of Christ be transferred to them. Fill them with the sin-conquering life of Jesus that is in the blood, so that the Spirit of Christ may be imparted to them, that they may repent, rethink, change, and go and sin no more. I call to Your remembrance the divine potential, promise, and destiny You have created within _____ . Help them fulfill their God-given purpose and glorify You, in Jesus' name. Amen.*

"Applying the blood" of the Passover protection

Pleading and *applying* the blood are not the same. Pleading is interceding, but applying the blood invokes the *Passover protection*. This is

---

[6] 1 John 5:16

[7] Exodus 19:6, Revelation 1:6, 5:10

[8] Hebrews 10:19–22

the Biblical basis for establishing a "bloodline" of protection around believers. Sometimes people use the word "plead" when they refer to "applying" the Passover blood to their homes and lives.[9]

The original Passover in Egypt required putting the blood of a lamb on the doorposts of every Israelite house. When the death angel saw the blood, he had to "pass over" (skip) that house. The Egyptians, whose houses were not protected by blood, lost their firstborn child and the firstborn of their animals.

Jesus is your "Passover Lamb,"[10] seeing He was crucified during the Passover feast. Spiritually applying His blood to your house lights a neon sign in the spirit realm, declaring to every evil spirit that this "house" (body or household) is protected by God. It creates a bloodline of protection around your house and property. As the Passover blood kept the destroyer from killing the firstborn in Egypt, the spiritual presence of the blood of Christ protects you and your household.

Apply the blood with the full authority of one having the right to speak in the name of Jesus. Go to the doorposts of your house (the points of entry) and spiritually "apply" the blood to the sides and tops of the doorframes. Speak your faith aloud in Jesus' name. Believe God is hearing your prayers and setting up a protective perimeter around your house. If you like, apply a touch of olive oil to represent the blood. Do the same at the corners of your property and its points of entry. This creates the "bloodline" around your family and property.

> *Father, I apply the blood of Jesus, my Passover Lamb, to the doorposts of my life and family. I apply the blood to my house and property lines and forbid the destroyer to enter my gates. I apply the blood to my finances, bank accounts, and place of work. I thank you that Your Spirit hovers over my family and protects us. (When driving) I apply the blood to my vehicle, front to back, side to side, top to bottom, to the driver and all passengers, and ask that You keep us safe from other drivers and vehicles and move all animals off the road. In Jesus' name. Amen.*

---

[9]   Exodus 12:3–7, 23

[10] 1 Corinthians 5:7

As powerful as the blood is, we find another secret advantage in the light of Christ—the indwelling guidance of the Holy Spirit.

SECRET #9: When you *plead* the blood of Christ in intercession, God sends the Holy Spirit to lead the one for whom you pray to repentance and faith in Christ, that they may receive forgiveness of sins and the power to go and sin no more. When you *apply* the Passover blood, you create a "bloodline" of protection around those you love.

CHAPTER TEN

The Spirit Leads Us to Dwell Safely

And He led them on safely, so that they did not fear;
But the sea overwhelmed their enemies. —Psalm 78:53

Part of spiritual warfare is living in divine protection. You can't do anything for God if you are dead. Terrorism and random violence have become common in our country in recent years. As a result, we pray to God for safety. The Lord's plan to protect His people is based on the following principle: *It's easier for God to move His children out of harm's way than to stop rebellious people from doing evil.*

As we saw in Chapter 7 on "Why You Must Pray," God reigns over the earth and will hold all men accountable for their actions on the Day of Judgment. But people still have free will, and some refuse to listen to Him and do terrible things to others. Because the Lord gave mankind freedom of choice, He does not exercise direct control over everything that happens on earth.[1] This means that obedience to the Lord and proper timing on our part are keys to avoiding potentially dangerous

---

[1] Genesis 4:5–8. Before Cain killed Abel, God visited Cain and entreated him to control the anger lurking at his door like a wild beast. But Cain was free to make his own choice. The Lord did *not* further intervene by sending an angel to restrain Cain before he committed earth's first murder. In this test tube case, God permitted man's free will choice even though it was a bad one. To this day, God counsels every man's heart to do right, but if he disobeys, his evil choice will ultimately be judged. While men are free to make choices, they cannot pick their consequences.

people and situations. To stay safe in a crazy world, we must become sensitive to and led by God's Spirit.[2]

How will the Lord move you away from danger? First, He knows more than the FBI, the CIA, or Homeland Security. He sees ahead of time what will happen. Because of His love for us, He conveys "inside information" to His listening children by the Holy Spirit—a distinct advantage to being a born-again child of God. The world calls this having a hunch or a "sixth sense," but the Bible calls it a "word of knowledge,"[3] a spontaneous revelation by the Spirit of God of a fact known to the mind of God but unknown to the recipient.

For example, Jesus warned the early Christians years in advance to flee to the mountains when they saw the Roman army march against Jerusalem. Those who obeyed were spared. Through Moses, the Lord warned the children of Israel to move away from the tents of Korah before the earth opened and swallowed them. Those who obeyed Moses lived; those who refused died.

Stories surfaced from the 9/11 tragedy of people who were led not to go to work that day in the twin towers. Others could not go for various reasons or were delayed, and their lives were spared. God did what He could to protect people, and the number of lives lost was far less than anyone would have expected. Terrorist acts are no surprise to God, and He warns and helps people avoid eminent danger. Our job is to watch, pray, listen, and obey.

The Lord told an unnamed prophet in the Old Testament to deliver a message in a certain place and leave, not eating bread or drinking water or returning by the same route. When he delayed to eat and drink, a lion later met him on the road and killed him.[4] Had he obeyed God's instructions in a timely way, he would have avoided the lion crossing his path.

God warned the wise men who brought gifts to the young child Jesus not to return to Herod. By obeying, they protected Jesus' life and possibly their own.[5] Paul was forbidden by the Holy Spirit to preach the

---

[2]   Romans 8:14

[3]   1 Corinthians 12:8

[4]   1 Kings 13:9, 23–24

[5]   Matthew 2:11–12

Word in Asia and Bithynia.[6] Only the Holy Spirit knew what trouble or possible death awaited them there. When He guided them to Macedonia, they had much success.

People with prophetic gifts and proven track records sometimes give words of warning. For example, Elisha the prophet warned the king of Israel of traps set for him by the king of Syria.[7] Agabus warned Paul of impending imprisonment.[8] But these are exceptions and not the rule for the following reason.

> ### It's easier for God to move His children out of harm's way than to stop rebellious people from doing evil.

The main person God speaks to about your life is you. The Holy Spirit lives in you, and your job is to obey His inner promptings. The Lord will nudge you where to go, which route to take, when it's okay to stay, and when it's time to go. But the question is: are you flexible enough to override your habitual way of doing things if the Lord so impresses you? His promptings do not come with trumpet blasts but as a still, small voice. Do you have to drive the same way home every day? So what if one takes five minutes longer and has two more traffic signals? Be adaptable and open to variety. *Pray before you do things and listen for God's promptings.* He will guide you around accidents, dangerous people, and other hazards.

Another gift of the Holy Spirit is discerning of spirits.[9] Have you ever talked to someone when "red flags" went up, warning you of something not right there? Have you ever experienced a "check in your spirit" about a certain person or place? Through this gift, God warns His people and keeps them safe from deception.

Practice being led by the Holy Spirit in the small things, so you're ready for bigger things. When in the grocery store, ask the Lord if you've forgotten anything. If He impresses you to buy milk, do it. You may think

---

6   Acts 16:6–10
7   2 Kings 6:8–12
8   Acts 21:10–11
9   1 Corinthians 12:10

you have enough, but when you get home you could find out the kids drank it or an unexpected guest is staying for dinner. Learn to be sensitive to the inner hunch or voice.

Scripture promises that when the Holy Spirit is poured out on us we will live securely in peaceful places.

> Until at last the Spirit is poured out
>   on us from heaven.
> Then the wilderness will become a fertile field,
>   and the fertile field will yield bountiful crops.
> Justice will rule in the wilderness
>   and righteousness in the fertile field.
> And this righteousness will bring peace.
>   Yes, it will bring quietness and confidence forever.
> My people will live in safety, quietly at home.
>   They will be at rest.
>
> —Isaiah 32:15–18 (NLT)

Father, Your Word declares that as many as are led by the Spirit of God are the sons and daughters of God. Safely lead and guide my family and myself by Your Holy Spirit. Help us become sensitive to Your still small voice. Help us be flexible and adjust our plans as You impress us. Help us not to be led by fear but to walk boldly in faith. In Jesus' name, I pray. Amen.

Next, we'll see how wisdom should be our best friend and wonderful counselor.

SECRET #10: Allow yourself to be guided out of harm's way by the promptings of the Holy Spirit. Stay in tune by abiding in the secret place with the Lord, watching, praying, listening, and obeying.

CHAPTER ELEVEN

Wisdom Delivers from Trouble

Then I saw that wisdom excels folly
As light excels darkness. —Ecclesiastes 2:13

Wisdom is another key to divine protection. Sometimes we call it common sense, although it's not that common. Wisdom cries aloud in public places and warns us to avoid the people, places, and practices that get us into trouble.[1]

> Do not enter the path of the wicked,
> And do not walk in the way of evil.
> Avoid it, do not travel on it;
> Turn away from it and pass on.
>
> *—Proverbs 4:14–15*

For example, if we drive while drunk or high on drugs or ride with someone under the influence, we put our life in harm's way. Don't go places with people you don't know or don't trust unless the Lord leads you. Wisdom wrote the proverb, "If a bird sees a trap being set, it knows to stay away."[2] Are birds smarter than people? Can't we see the traps that are set for us?

Here's another one: "A prudent man foresees evil and hides himself, but the simple pass on and are punished."[3] Our personal choices prove

---

[1] 1 Corinthians 15:33
[2] Proverbs 1:17 (NLT)
[3] Proverbs 22:3

to everyone whether we are wise or foolish. Wisdom can protect us only if we are willing to hear.

> *Father, fill me with wisdom and discernment that I may associate with the right people and avoid the occasions of sin. Give me the foresight to see where an activity or an association will take me that I may turn away from evil. In Jesus' name, I pray. Amen.*

Proverbs highlights our need for wisdom in simple, practical statements. For example, "The fear of the Lord is the beginning of wisdom."[4] We avoid trouble when we pay attention to the voice of wisdom.

"But whoever listens to me will dwell safely,
And will be secure, without fear of evil."

—Proverbs 1:33

For the LORD grants wisdom!
From his mouth come knowledge and understanding.
He grants a treasure of common sense to the honest.
He is a shield to those who walk with integrity.

—Proverbs 2:6–7 (NLT)

Wisdom will save you from evil people,
from those whose words are twisted.

—Proverbs 2:12 (NLT)

Wisdom will save you from the immoral woman,
from the seductive words of the promiscuous woman.
She has abandoned her husband
and ignores the covenant she made before God.
Entering her house leads to death;
it is the road to the grave.

—Proverbs 2:16–18 (NLT)

My child, don't lose sight of common sense and discernment.
Hang on to them,
for they will refresh your soul.
They are like jewels on a necklace.
They keep you safe on your way,

---

4 Proverbs 9:10

and your feet will not stumble.
You can go to bed without fear;
    you will lie down and sleep soundly.
You need not be afraid of sudden disaster
    or the destruction that comes upon the wicked,
for the LORD is your security.
He will keep your foot from being caught in a trap.

                  —Proverbs 3:21–26 (NLT)

"Don't turn your back on wisdom, for she will protect you.
    Love her, and she will guard you.
Getting wisdom is the wisest thing you can do!
    And whatever else you do, develop good judgment.
If you prize wisdom, she will make you great.
    Embrace her, and she will honor you.
She will place a lovely wreath on your head;
    she will present you with a beautiful crown."

                  —Proverbs 4:6–9 (NLT)

Wisdom will multiply your days
    and add years to your life.

                  —Proverbs 9:11 (NLT)

Value the advice of godly parents, good friends, and the wisdom of the Word of God, and apply what you hear. "Tie [their words] around your neck."[5] Pray that past hurts not cause you to rebel against the sound counsel of those who care for you.

Let light and understanding and excellent wisdom be found in you as they were in Daniel.[6] In our next chapter, we'll learn the value of proactive Christian living.

SECRET #11: Wisdom is a key to divine safety, but foolishness opens you to trouble and sorrow. Make wisdom your friend and associate with wise people, and you will become wise.

---

[5] Proverbs 3:3
[6] Daniel 5:14

CHAPTER TWELVE

What to Do Before the Battle

Let the praises of God be in their mouths,
And a sharp sword in their hands. —Psalm 149:6

Praising God has protective power. In one battle recorded in the Old Testament, King Jehoshaphat placed singers and praisers in front of the army as they went to battle. Sounds a little crazy, right? But King Jehoshaphat realized something many don't, that the Lord *leads* His troops into battle[1] in front of the army. Putting musicians closest to where He was made spiritual sense. The tactic worked, as God's presence[2] so unnerved the enemy that they fought among themselves and fled before Israel arrived. Songs of praise won the battle before anyone shot an arrow.

> And when he had consulted with the people, he appointed those who should sing to the LORD, and who should praise the beauty of holiness, as they went out before the army and were saying: "Praise the LORD, For His mercy endures forever."
> —*2 Chronicles 20:21 (italics added)*

We apply this principle when we pray, praise, and sing on the way to battle. *Pray proactively!* Ask the Lord to go before you, praising Him as

---

[1] Deuteronomy 31:8, 3, Exodus 13:21
[2] Psalm 22:3

you go, for this releases His power. When you arrive, things will be under control. It's easy to overlook the power in praise, but a simple reading of the Psalms convinces us of its strategic value.

> Let the saints be joyful in glory;
> Let them sing aloud on their beds.
> Let the high praises of God be in their mouth,
> And a two-edged sword in their hand.
>
> *—Psalm 149:5–6*

> Out of the mouth of babes and nursing infants
> You have ordained strength,
> Because of Your enemies,
> That You may silence the enemy and the avenger.
>
> *—Psalm 8:2*

Jesus quoted Psalm 8:2 like this, "Out of the mouth of babes and nursing infants You have *perfected praise*."[3] Praise silences the voice of the enemy and the avenger. While you sing, the enemy cannot attack your mind. Praise mutes the enemy's voice and draws the Spirit of God to you. Try it for yourself. Not only are the bad voices muted, but praising God changes the atmosphere around you, attracts the angels, and drives the enemy away.

> But you are a chosen generation, a royal priesthood, a holy nation,
> His own special people, that you may proclaim the praises of Him who
> called you out of darkness into His marvelous light;
>
> *—1 Peter 2:9*

In World War II, the military used aircraft and the big guns on battleships to "soften up" the beaches before any GI's landed. Praying in advance softens up the enemy's defenses. Pray strategically. Before that big family get together, pray that your relatives will not argue or drink too much. By sending the Lord ahead of you and binding disruptive influences, you'll have a more pleasant day.

Jesus always prayed in advance. On the way to Lazarus' tomb, He *groaned* within Himself.[4] The Greek word means *to snort with anger* like

---

[3] Matthew 21:16
[4] John 11:33, 38

a horse, *to be strongly moved, to rebuke sternly.* As He walked, Jesus rebuked death and commanded life and healing into Lazarus' body. At the tomb He ordered them to remove the stone to see what prayer had accomplished—Lazarus was alive again! In the garden of Gethsemane during the most critical hour, Jesus prayed for strength to endure without sin, knowing He was to be mocked, flogged, and crucified.

God is the God of the future and preplans for every event. We call Him Jehovah-Jireh because He sees ahead and provides for our needs before we know we have the need. If an unforeseen circumstance surprises you, don't panic. It's no surprise to God. He saw it coming long before it happened. Pray and look around you. God has a "ram caught in the bushes" waiting to be found.[5] Your job is to seek until you find it.

> ### *Praise silences the voice of the enemy and the avenger. While you are singing, the enemy cannot attack your mind.*

As Christians, we love to quote Romans 8:28, "And we know that all things work together for good to those who love God, to those who are the called according to His purpose." A man of God once explained that verse 28 operates because of verse 26, the Holy Spirit praying through us at a deep level. All things work together for good *when we pray!*

> *Heavenly Father, I will pray and praise You before every situation so you may move on my behalf. Let the Holy Spirit prepare the way before me. In Jesus' name, I pray. Amen.*

Praising and praying are two ways that help us abide under the shadow of the Almighty, which we'll learn more about next.

SECRET #12: Pray and praise on your way to the battle, knowing the Lord goes in front of you, prepares the way before you, and fights the battle for you.

---

5   Genesis 22:12–14

CHAPTER THIRTEEN

Abiding under the Shadow of the Almighty

For the LORD God is a sun and shield;
The LORD will give grace and glory;
No good thing will He withhold
From those who walk uprightly.
—Psalm 84:11

A shepherd boy's fearless words of faith brought him before the king. The leader was disappointed when he saw him, supposing the one willing to fight the giant intimidating Israel would be a seasoned warrior, not a lad. As the king pointed out his youthful inexperience, the young man answered boldly. He described how he had fought a lion and a bear while protecting his father's sheep. Obviously, he had reflexes like lightning and was cool in the face of danger.

> "Your servant has killed both lion and bear; and this uncircumcised Philistine will be like one of them, seeing he has defied the armies of the living God." Moreover David said, "The LORD, who delivered me from the paw of the lion and from the paw of the bear, He will deliver me from the hand of this Philistine." And Saul said to David, "Go, and the LORD be with you!"
>
> *—1 Samuel 17:36–37*

Thus began one of the Bible's most famous passages, the story of young David slaying Goliath, the nine-foot-tall Philistine giant. It was a profile in courage that was born of David's faith that God delivers those who serve Him.

The secret of David's faith

David looked at the conflict differently than everyone else: "For who is this *uncircumcised* Philistine, that he should defy the armies of the living God?"[1] What did circumcision have to do with the outcome of a battle? To David, everything! His personal circumcision was *a sign of his covenant with God,*[2] which made the Lord his shield and ally. Divine help and protection were real to him, but the uncircumcised Goliath had no such covenant.[3] With God's help, David ran to the battle, hurled a stone from his sling, killed the giant, and cut off his head.

In fighting to defend his sheep and his nation, David understood the Lord's shepherd heart for His people. Some say Psalm 23, composed by David, is the best-known passage of the Bible worldwide. The Lord is our ever-present Shepherd, feeding, caring for, and protecting His sheep in this life and into eternity.

> Yea, though I walk through the valley of the shadow of
>   death,
> I will fear no evil;
> For You are with me;
> Your rod and Your staff, they comfort me.
>
> —*Psalm 23:4*

King David took God as his shield

The divine shield promised to Abraham was real to David. Time after time as a warrior, he was victorious in man-to-man combat. He sang of the shield in the Psalms, claiming God's promise to Abraham and his descendants as his own. Here are some of my favorite passages.

> The LORD is my rock and my fortress and my deliverer;
> The God of my strength, in whom I will trust;
> My *shield* and the horn of my salvation,

---

[1] 1 Samuel 17:26

[2] Genesis 17:1–2, 7–14

[3] Cp. Numbers 14:9

My stronghold and my refuge;
My Savior, You save me from violence.

—2 Samuel 22:2–3 (italics added)

As for God, His way is perfect;
The word of the LORD is proven;
He is a *shield* to all who trust in Him.

—2 Samuel 22:31 (italics added)

You have also given me the *shield* of Your salvation;
Your gentleness has made me great.

—2 Samuel 22:36 (italics added)

But You, O LORD, are a *shield* for me,
My glory and the One who lifts up my head.

—Psalm 3:3 (italics added)

For You, O LORD, will bless the righteous;
With favor You will surround him as with a *shield*.

—Psalm 5:12 (italics added)

The LORD is my strength and my *shield*;
My heart trusted in Him, and I am helped;
Therefore my heart greatly rejoices,
And with my song I will praise Him.

—Psalm 28:7 (italics added)

For the LORD God is a sun and *shield*;
The LORD will give grace and glory;
No good thing will He withhold
From those who walk uprightly.

—Psalm 84:11 (italics added)

To David, the overshadowing presence of God was his shield, protecting him from evil like a child wrapped in the arms of his parent.

Oh, how great is Your goodness,
Which You have laid up for those who fear You,
Which You have prepared for those who trust in You
In the presence of the sons of men!
You shall hide them in the secret place of Your presence

From the plots of man;
You shall keep them secretly in a pavilion
From the strife of tongues.

—*Psalm 31:19–20 (italics added)*

Other writers believed in God's sheltering care as well.

The name of the LORD is a strong tower;
The righteous run to it and are safe.

—*Proverbs 18:10*

I will lift up my eyes to the hills—
From whence comes my help?
My help comes from the LORD,
Who made heaven and earth.
He will not allow your foot to be moved;
He who keeps you will not slumber.
Behold, He who keeps Israel
Shall neither slumber nor sleep.
The LORD is your keeper;
The LORD is your shade at your right hand.
The sun shall not strike you by day,
Nor the moon by night.
The LORD shall preserve you from all evil;
He shall preserve your soul.
The LORD shall preserve your going out and your coming in
 From this time forth, and even forevermore.

—*Psalm 121*

When you lie down, you will not be afraid;
Yes, you will lie down and your sleep will be sweet.

—*Proverbs 3:24*

The covenant God made with Abraham and his seed was still in place centuries later. In 701 B.C., Sennacherib, the Assyrian conqueror, laid siege to Jerusalem during the reign of King Hezekiah. One night the angel of the Lord killed one hundred and eighty-five thousand Assyrian troops, forcing the army to withdraw. The Lord fought for His people,[4]

---

[4]   2 Kings 19:35, 2 Chronicles 32:21

and He will again! Today's leaders in Israel need constant faith in God's promise to Abraham, "I am your shield, your exceedingly great reward."

Psalm 91's wonderful promises

Psalm 91 outlines the wonderful protections belonging to those in covenant with the Lord.

> *He who dwells in the secret place of the Most High*
> *Shall abide under the shadow of the Almighty.*
> I will say of the LORD, *"He is my refuge and my fortress;*
> My God, in Him I will trust."

Surely He shall deliver you from the snare of the fowler
And from the perilous pestilence.
He shall cover you with His feathers,
And under His wings you shall take refuge;
His truth shall be your shield and buckler.
You shall not be afraid of the terror by night,
Nor of the arrow that flies by day,
Nor of the pestilence that walks in darkness,
Nor of the destruction that lays waste at noonday.

A thousand may fall at your side,
And ten thousand at your right hand;
But it shall not come near you.
Only with your eyes shall you look,
And see the reward of the wicked.

Because you have made the Lord, who is my refuge,
Even the Most High, your dwelling place,
No evil shall befall you,
Nor shall any plague come near your dwelling;
For He shall give His angels charge over you,
To keep you in all your ways.
In their hands they shall bear you up,
Lest you dash your foot against a stone.
You shall tread upon the lion and the cobra,
The young lion and the serpent you shall trample underfoot.

"Because he has set his love upon Me, therefore I will deliver
   him;
I will set him on high, because he has known My name.
He shall call upon Me, and I will answer him;
I will be with him in trouble;
I will deliver him and honor him.
With long life I will satisfy him,
And show him My salvation."

—Psalm 91:1–16 (italics added)

To David, the overshadowing presence of God was his shield, protecting him from evil like a child wrapped in the arms of his parent.

Spiritual protection comes from dwelling under the shadow of the Almighty, like chicks seeking shelter under their mother's wings. The Lord becomes our dwelling place and refuge when we keep much company with Him. Jesus called this *abiding*. We are to abide in Him and allow Him and His Word to abide in us.[5] We abide or dwell in the secret place by carving out time from our schedules for God, church, worship, prayer, and meditation in His Word.

God promised different types of protection to those who dwell in the secret place. He protects us from…

- *"the snare of the fowler"* (v. 3): sin and temptation, the stumbling blocks, foot-snares, and deathtraps of the enemy

- *"the perilous pestilence"* (v. 3): infectious diseases and plagues

- *"the terror by night"* (v. 5): thieves, evildoers, and terrorists who come by night, including sickness and nightmares

- *"the arrow that flies by day"* (v. 5): arrows, spears, bullets, missiles, rockets, including flaming thought arrows

- *"the pestilence that walks in darkness"* (v. 6): such as killed the firstborn of Egypt

---

[5] John 8:31–32, 15:1–8

- *"the destruction that lays waste at noonday"* (v. 6): that which destroys, such as terrorist bombs
- *"no evil...nor any plague"* (v. 10): accident, misfortune, injury, plague, or disease
- *"lion...cobra...young lion...serpent"* (v. 13): wild animals and "wild things" in the spirit realm

Read Psalm 91 daily, especially if you serve in the military or law enforcement, work in a dangerous environment, live in an unsafe neighborhood, are afraid of being alone at night, or want to calm your heart about random acts of violence. Keep its promises fresh within you. They will protect you from terror or fear, the purpose behind acts of terrorism. Calmness in the face of danger lets the enemy know he has failed.

> Don't be afraid of your enemies; always be courageous, and this will prove to them that they will lose and that you will win, because it is God who gives you the victory.
>
> —*Philippians 1:28 (GNT)*

God demonstrated His protection in the Passover

The Lord demonstrated the power of His safekeeping during the ten plagues in Egypt. Pharaoh kept refusing to let the people go, so Moses told him beginning with the fourth plague that God would "set apart the land of Goshen" where Israel lived.

> "And in that day *I will set apart the land of Goshen,* in which My people dwell, that no swarms of flies shall be there, in order that you may know that I am the LORD in the midst of the land. *I will make a difference between My people and your people.* Tomorrow this sign shall be."
>
> —*Exodus 8:22–23 (italics added)*

No swarms of flies were found in Goshen. The livestock of Egypt died in the fifth plague while not one of Israel's livestock died. Egypt was pounded with hail in the seventh plague, but there was no hail in Goshen. Thick darkness covered Egypt for three days in the ninth plague, but the children of Israel had light.[6]

---

[6]   Exodus 9:6, 26, 10:22–23

The tenth and final plague was the death of the firstborn in all Egypt. God gave Israel special instructions for their protection. They were to apply the blood of a lamb to the doorposts of their houses. God's Spirit would "pass over" (or hover over) those houses marked with blood and not allow the destroying angel to enter them.[7] Israel was shielded by a lamb's blood, and their children were spared. The Passover was a *covenant blessing,* and it made a life-and-death difference.

Jesus is our Passover Lamb, crucified at the Passover Feast. When we accept Him as Savior, His blood is applied to the doorposts of our lives. We are marked and "passed over" in the evil day. Just as David faced the giant and prevailed, we who put our faith in Jesus are shielded and protected, living in the light of God's favor. In the next chapter, we'll talk more about dwelling in the secret place.

> *Father, I have made a covenant with You through Jesus Christ, and I trust You to deliver me and my household. You are the Good Shepherd, caring for and protecting Your sheep. Because I dwell in the secret place of the Most High, I claim the protections listed in Psalm 91. No evil shall befall me, neither shall any plague come near my dwelling. For You have given Your angels charge over me. I have applied the blood of the Lamb Jesus to the doorposts of our house. You make a difference between us and the world in the evil day as You did for Israel during the plagues. Thank You for passing over and defending us in the day of calamity. We love You, Father, and thank You for the wonderful blessings of divine protection, in Jesus' name. Amen.*

SECRET #13: When you make time to dwell in the secret place of the Most High, you abide under the shadow of the Almighty. As He did for David and Israel, God covers you and your family with the shield of His presence.

---

[7] Exodus 12:23

CHAPTER FOURTEEN

Dwelling in the Secret Place of the Most High

He who dwells in the secret place of the Most High
Shall abide under the shadow of the Almighty.
—Psalm 91:1

When I was a child, I was fascinated with forts, making blanket forts every chance I got. When outside, my friends and I hacked our way into the willow thickets that lined the river nearby and built forts inside them. I loved the protective feeling of being hidden by a canopy, whether blankets or tree branches.

As we saw in the last chapter, Psalm 91 described something similar. "He who dwells in the secret place of the Most High shall abide under the shadow of the Almighty." Dwelling in the secret place of the Most High is like being in a fort with God's presence covering us. The secret place is the ultimate place of protection, as He alone is our refuge and fortress. Below are a few passages that contain the word translated "secret place" in Psalm 91, sometimes rendered "hiding place." The Lord wants to hide you in your time of trouble.

> For in the time of trouble
> He shall hide me in His pavilion;
> In the *secret place* of His tabernacle

He shall hide me;
He shall set me high upon a rock.

—Psalm 27:5 (italics added)

You are my *hiding place;*
You shall preserve me from trouble;

You shall surround me with songs of deliverance.
Selah

—Psalm 32:7 (italics added)

You are my *hiding place* and my shield;
I hope in Your word.

—Psalm 119:114 (italics added)

The secret place is also called a "refuge."

God is our *refuge* and strength,
A very present help in trouble.

—Psalm 46:1 (italics added)

In God is my salvation and my glory;
The rock of my strength,
And my *refuge*, is in God.
Trust in Him at all times, you people;
Pour out your heart before Him;
God is a *refuge* for us. Selah

—Psalm 62:7–8 (italics added)

But the LORD has been my defense,
And my God the rock of my *refuge*.

—Psalm 94:22 (italics added)

I cried out to You, O LORD:
I said, "You are my *refuge*,
My portion in the land of the living."

—Psalm 142:5 (italics added)

And there will be a tabernacle for shade in the daytime from
the heat, for a place of *refuge*, and for a shelter from storm
and rain.

—Isaiah 4:6 (italics added)

Protected by faith, not works

But how can I dwell in the secret place with the One who will ulti-mately judge my life? If I am continually striving to earn merit points to outweigh my ongoing failures, what assurance do I have that He will accept me? Can my flawed notions of holiness please an absolutely per-fect and holy God? The truth is—they can't. My faith is paralyzed if I think I have to be *good enough* to work my way into God's presence.

Christianity is unique among the world's religions, including Juda-ism, in that access to the secret place with God is not earned by good deeds, by performing outward religious acts, or by being born into a high priestly family. Christians come into right relationship with God by *believing* in the perfect sacrifice Jesus made for sins, not through our human works. It's an altogether free gift of righteousness.

> *Christ's sacrifice makes it possible for imperfect human beings to dwell in the secret place of the Most High, fully accepted by God.*

In a "works" system, a person can never experience soul peace, never being assured he has done enough. But Christ offers peace through simple faith in what *He* did as the perfect Son of God. Would you rather base your faith on your imperfect human performance or on what Jesus did for you? Being "religious" and doing "religious works" can never make a man good enough, but faith in Christ does, because *His righteousness* is imputed to us.

> God saved you by his grace when you believed. And you can't take credit for this; it is a gift from God. Salvation is not a reward for the good things we have done, so none of us can boast about it.
>
> —*Ephesians 2:8–9 (NLT)*

Therefore, since we have been made right in God's sight by faith, we have peace with God because of what Jesus Christ our Lord has done for us.

—Romans 5:1 (NLT)

"Come to Me, all you who labor and are heavy laden, and I will give you rest. Take My yoke upon you and learn from Me, for I am gentle and lowly in heart, and you will find rest for your souls. For My yoke is easy and My burden is light."

—Jesus Christ, Matthew 11:28–30

The shadow of an ice cream cone

Not long ago, I walked into an ice cream shop permeated with the warm fragrance of freshly-baked waffle cones. My wife and I were innocently walking down the street when we were accosted by these wonderful aromas and followed our noses through the open door from which these enticing scents were coming.

Perhaps you enjoy ice cream, too, at least once in a while. Take a moment to imagine your favorite flavor in a freshly-baked waffle cone. What you are thinking about now (the shadow or thought of the ice cream cone) is good, but tasting the flavorful, crunchy, creamy, calorie-laden, real thing is better. The shadow cone is less fattening, and you can eat as much as you want, but it's also less satisfying.

The old covenant given by Moses was the "shadow"[1] of the new covenant. It was good, instructive, and enlightening, the brightest revelation of its day. Only one thing could supersede it—the fulfillment of the very things it foreshadowed! The glorious new covenant completed the Old and offered one huge advantage—it had a new administrator—Mr. Faith. Mr. Faith had been the original administrator of the covenant, but Mr. Law was placed in charge at the time of Moses. Unfortunately, no man could ever live up to what Mr. Law demanded. When Jesus the Messiah came and fulfilled the law, Mr. Law stepped down, his job being done. Mr. Faith heads up the covenant again, which is administered by *faith* in what Jesus did, not by a law that measures what men do.

---

[1]   Hebrews 8:5, 10:1, Colossians 2:17

If the old way [the law of Moses], which brings condemnation, was glorious, how much more glorious is the new way [obtained through faith in Christ], which makes us right with God! In fact, that first glory was not glorious at all compared with the overwhelming glory of the new way. So if the old way, which has been replaced, was glorious, how much more glorious is the new, which remains forever!

—*2 Corinthians 3:9–11 (NLT)*

Nesting in the "secret place"

In Christ we are privileged to know God as Father. We no longer cringe before Him as Judge because Jesus bore the punishment of all sin for us. Christ's sacrifice makes it possible for imperfect human beings to dwell in the secret place of the Most High, fully accepted by God.[2] Our access to the secret place is based on Christ's sacrifice, so there is no limit to the Psalm 91 protection we can receive. We don't have to be perfect to experience the protection of God. Access to the secret place is a covenant blessing.

> *Our access to the secret place is based on Christ's sacrifice, so there is no limit to the Psalm 91 protection we can receive.*

We need a safe place to flee for safety where we can commune intimately and personally with the Lord. For me, it happens at the breakfast counter first thing in the morning as I read God's Word and pray. I need wisdom daily, and it comes to me as I seek Him in my secret place. In that wisdom is both guidance and protection.

Have you ever watched a bird make a nest? It gathers sticks, grass, and feathers from its own breast to create a soft, protected place to lay its eggs. Your secret place with God is made like a bird's nest. It fits you perfectly and gets softer every day as you arrange it to suit yourself. In your secret place you gather your Bibles, devotionals, books you are reading, and your notetaker. You bring an open heart and an open ear. You pray

---

[2]   Ephesians 1:6

and welcome the Lord to join you and share a time of personal communion. The more time you spend in your secret place, the more it becomes home to you, and the more at home you become with the Lord.

Abiding in the secret place with God is how we grow in faith and receive guidance. As we seek to hear from Him, He pitches His canopy of protection over us like a tent. Mary became pregnant with Jesus as the power of the Holy Spirit overshadowed her like a canopy. While abiding in Him, we may become pregnant with divine callings, life missions, and guidance for all things. Enlightenment takes place as we open ourselves to His Spirit, abiding under the wings of the Almighty.

> *Father, draw me into the secret place with You, where I am accepted because of what Jesus did, not because of my own works. Show me how to rest in you and abide under the shadow of Your protective wings. Hide me in the secret place of Your presence from the plots of men and the strife of tongues. In Jesus' name, I pray. Amen.*

As we continue to learn how to live in the light, sometimes we overlook little things that make a huge impact. We'll talk about one of them in the next chapter. Controlling the tongue makes a huge difference in relationships and reduces the interpersonal friction we often interpret as spiritual warfare. Are you listening? It might not always be the devil; it might be the way you *said* something that stirred people up in a wrong way. Spending time in the secret place will help you choose your words more carefully.

SECRET #14: Remember, access to the secret place of the Most High is not for those whose works are perfect, but for you who have been made righteous by faith in Jesus' blood. As you abide under the shadow of the Lord's wings, His fortress of protection shelters you.

CHAPTER FIFTEEN

Winning the Battle of the Tongue

And the tongue is a fire, a world of iniquity. The tongue is so set among our members that it defiles the whole body, and sets on fire the course of nature; and it is set on fire by hell. —James 3:6

I became a Christian three months out of college (where we vigorously debated everything), and I had to grow up. At that time I spoke my mind with few filters and little concern as to how my words affected others. In a conflict, thoughts popped into my head about how to respond. When I spoke them, the conflict usually escalated.

I remember one discussion ending with silent pain in the other person's eyes. While I had emphatically made my point, the young man I was witnessing to would never willingly talk to me again. I soon recognized that evil, real evil, was present in strife, and its goal was to destroy my relationships. Unfortunately, I was all too willing to cooperate.

One night I dreamed I was watching a stage play in a theater. A family of four sat at the dinner table. My point of view was directly over the stage where the light bars were. From my vantage point I saw an odd thing: each person at the table had strings attached to them, like they were marionettes, only they weren't puppets but real people. Perched high on the light bars above the stage, hidden from the audience, were four nondescript, blob-like creatures. With their hands they controlled the strings connected to each person. Quietly and methodically during the meal, the blobs pulled on the strings that influenced what each person said—until that nice family dinner turned into a shouting match.

The dream was weird but vivid and clear, and it spoke a message to my heart. Though I could not see them with my natural eyes, I realized there were invisible things that pulled my strings and pushed my buttons to make me say things I would later regret. I concluded that I must take control of my mouth, to wait, think, and pray before I spoke, and when in doubt to keep my mouth shut. It appeared that spiritual forces I never thought existed were attempting to use my mouth to destroy my relationships and were succeeding, at least, in doing damage.

Though strange, the dream did not disturb me. God reveals truth without glorifying the dark side. He showed just enough about the "blobs" for me to know what I needed to do. I didn't have to be an expert in darkness to realize I needed to control my tongue. Paul wished Christians were wise concerning good and innocent when it came to evil.[1] Jesus said we are to be "wise as serpents and harmless as doves."[2]

The big problem with the little tongue

James wrote that the tongue is the most powerful member of the body and can be "set on fire by hell." We've all been scarred by negative words, and with our tongues perhaps we have scarred others. Controlling your tongue should be one of your highest priorities.

The Bible has much to say about words. Death and life are in the power of the tongue. The words we speak either build people up or tear people down. An uncontrolled tongue is like a weapon unleashed.

> Likewise, the tongue is a small part of the body, but it makes great boasts. Consider what a great forest is set on fire by a small spark. The tongue also is a fire, a world of evil among the parts of the body. It corrupts the whole body, sets the whole course of one's life on fire, and is itself set on fire by hell. All kinds of animals, birds, reptiles and sea creatures are being tamed and have been tamed by mankind, but no human being can tame the tongue. It is a restless evil, full of deadly poison. With the tongue we praise our Lord and Father, and with it we curse human beings, who have been made in God's likeness. Out of the same mouth come praise and cursing. My brothers and sisters, this should not be.
>
> —*James 3:5–10 (NIV)*

---

[1] Romans 16:19
[2] Matthew 10:16

My soul is among lions;
I lie among the sons of men
Who are set on fire,
Whose teeth are spears and arrows,
And their tongue a sharp sword.

—Psalm 57:4

The words of the reckless pierce like swords,
    but the tongue of the wise brings healing.

—Proverbs 12:18 (NIV)

Death and life are in the power of the tongue,
And those who love it will eat its fruit.

—Proverbs 18:21

He who guards his mouth preserves his life,
But he who opens wide his lips shall have destruction.

—Proverbs 13:3

"But I say to you that for every idle word men may speak, they will give account of it in the day of judgment. For by your words you will be justified, and by your words you will be condemned."

—Matthew 12:36–37

Putting a muzzle on my mouth

In my journey to control my tongue, the Psalms counseled me.

I said, "I will guard my ways,
Lest I sin with my tongue;
I will restrain my mouth with a muzzle,
While the wicked are before me."
I was mute with silence,
I held my peace even from good;
And my sorrow was stirred up.

—Psalm 39:1–2 (italics added)

Set a guard, O LORD, over my mouth;
Keep watch over the door of my lips.

—Psalm 141:3

Do not be like the horse or like the mule,
Which have no understanding,
Which must be harnessed with bit and bridle,
Else they will not come near you.

—Psalm 32:9

I imagined putting a muzzle on my mouth like people put on animals so they won't bite others. I learned to restrain myself, to "zip it up," so to speak. I imagined putting a bit and bridle in my mouth with the Holy Spirit holding the reins. We give account to the Lord for the words we speak, so we must rein in our tongues.

Being slow to speak allows us to gain control of what we are about to say before we hurt someone or put our foot in our mouth. If you've never practiced a day of silence, try it. It's harder than it sounds because we naturally blurt out thoughts without filtering them first. Deliberate silence helps break the "knee jerk," instantaneous connection between your thoughts and tongue. *You don't have to vocalize everything you think!* Practice holding your peace.

This reminds me of the old saying, "If you don't have anything good to say, say nothing at all." The Golden Rule says we should do to others as we wish they would do to us.[3] Shouldn't this apply to our speech? *Speak to others in the way you wish they would speak to you.*

The following proverb helped me a great deal.

A soft answer turns away wrath,
But a harsh word stirs up anger.

—Proverbs 15:1

When we respond gently and softly to someone losing their temper, it gives them a chance to cool down and control their tongue and tone of voice. Our soft answer will surprise them, and they will become embarrassed about being out of control. Our soft answer communicates, "If you are looking for a fight, you'll have to pick it with someone else."

Paul told us about the kinds of speech we are to put away from ourselves as Christians.

---

[3] Luke 6:31

> Therefore, putting away lying, "Let each one of you speak truth with his neighbor," for we are members of one another.
>
> —*Ephesians 4:25*

Lying is a sin against God, who is truth. It destroys trust, which is the building block of relationships with our family, neighbors, and friends.

> "Be angry, and do not sin": do not let the sun go down on your wrath, nor give place to the devil.
>
> —*Ephesians 4:26–27*

Anger gives the devil a place in us. When we lose control, he takes control. Look in the mirror when you are angry and upset; you won't look like yourself.

I imagined putting a bit and bridle in my mouth with the Holy Spirit holding the reins.

We are also to put away corrupt (bad or harmful) speech, bitterness, anger, noisy debate, and malice (hatred with thoughts of revenge).

> Do not let any unwholesome talk come out of your mouths, but only what is helpful for building others up according to their needs, that it may benefit those who listen. And do not grieve the Holy Spirit of God, with whom you were sealed for the day of redemption. Get rid of all bitterness, rage and anger, brawling and slander, along with every form of malice. Be kind and compassionate to one another, forgiving each other, just as in Christ God forgave you.
>
> —*Ephesians 4:29–32 (NIV)*

Be kind, tenderhearted, and forgiving like Jesus Christ.

Blessing and cursing from the same mouth

James explained, "Out of the same mouth proceed blessing and cursing."[4] We're double-minded if we bless people out of one side of our mouth and curse them out of the other. Perhaps certain words have

---

4   James 3:10

affected you your entire life: "You're no good." "You'll never amount to anything." "You're lazy (stupid, ugly, etc.)." Such "curses" did not come from your heavenly Father and are not what *He* thinks about you.

To Him you are made in the image of God, can do all things in Christ, and are as beautiful as a bride on her wedding day. We should never say such terrible things to our children, for if we do, we may scar them for life. We should always speak a positive blessing over them: "You are able." "You have what it takes." "You will be a success." "I'm so proud of you." Never speak negative words of death over yourself either: "I'm so stupid." "I can't do anything right." "I'll never be a success." "I'm not good at anything."

Though words have the power to destroy, they also have the potential to build up and impart grace.[5] Grace means undeserved favor that gives another chance, just as we hope others will do for us when we blow it. The mature person is the one who does not stumble in his words but is skilled at blessing others.

> We all stumble in many ways. Anyone who is never at fault in what they say is perfect, able to keep their whole body in check. When we put bits into the mouths of horses to make them obey us, we can turn the whole animal.
>
> —*James 3:2–3 (NIV)*

What kinds of things should we say?

The hallmarks of New Testament prophecy (speaking under the inspiration of the Holy Spirit) are *edification*, *exhortation*, and *comfort*.[6] Inspired speech ministers life and hope. Edification builds people up. Exhortation encourages and motivates. Comfort soothes hurts and eases pain. Prophetic words don't always begin, "Thus saith the Lord," nor do they always occur in church. You could be at work or in the grocery store and speak an inspired word of encouragement to someone. People are bruised enough by the world and their consciences, and most folks just need encouragement.

---

5   Colossians 4:6
6   1 Corinthians 14:3

Sound speech cannot be condemned.[7] Speaking the truth in love is maturity,[8] but nagging with the Word is a sign of immaturity. Paul counseled us to teach and admonish one another in psalms, hymns, and spiritual songs, singing with grace in our hearts to the Lord.[9]

These are tall orders for every member of the human race. Jesus taught that out of the abundance of the heart the mouth speaks.[10] If you don't like what is coming out of your mouth, then change what you meditate on in your heart. If you always think about the bad things a certain person did to you, then you will speak ill of them when opportunity arises. But when you meditate on the Word of God and your heart is filled with the Holy Spirit, then godly words, encouragement, wisdom, and praise will proceed from your mouth.

The battle of the tongue is a battle for maturity. If we don't control our tongues, the enemy will use us to speak damaging words even to those we profess to love. Relationships fall apart every day because of words. This is a battle every man and woman must win, for by control of the tongue we preserve our lives, marriages, and relationships.

Death and life are in the power of the tongue

Those who love to talk will eat the fruit of their words.[11] Words minister life and cause the people around us to blossom and grow, or words minister death and cause them to be hurt, wounded, and withdraw. Words are a blessing or a curse.

I once heard a sermon that described two kinds of people: accusers and intercessors. If we see something that is not right in someone, we respond in one of those two ways. We can be judgmental, legalistic, critical, and point out all their faults—and come off as an accuser—or we can intercede for them in prayer. Jesus commanded us to love others graciously as He loves us. He's never yet sat me down and chewed me out over everything I am doing wrong, but He does show me such love and grace that I want to correct myself.

---

[7]   Titus 2:8
[8]   Ephesians 4:15
[9]   Hebrews 13:15, Colossians 3:16
[10] Matthew 12:34
[11] Proverbs 18:21

Cancelling wrong words

All of us have said the wrong thing and hurt someone. What can we do? First, *we* must change. Saying "I'm sorry" is a start, but it isn't always enough. Sometimes we must admit, "I…was…wrong." Changing our behavior goes a long way toward procuring forgiveness. It makes "I'm sorry" mean something. Second, we can pray to cancel the power of the words we have spoken as well as those spoken against us.

Prayer to break harmful words spoken over us

Heavenly Father, you know the words spoken over me that cursed my life. You know the pain, humiliation, and damage they did to my self-esteem. But no word spoken by man is greater than the words You, as my Heavenly Father, speak over me. I believe who You say I am, what You say I have, and what You say I can do. I cancel the power of words that ignorant souls have spoken over me, and I declare that I am free from their power. I am who You made me to be, whether anyone else sees it or not. I love You, Father, and from now on I meditate on Your Words and let them build my self-image. Thank You for freeing me from the prison of words others have spoken over me. In Jesus' name. Amen.

Prayer to cancel the harmful words we have spoken

Heavenly Father, I repent of the damage I have done with my tongue. I cancel the power of the words with which I have cursed others. Please remove the memory of them from their minds and mine. Forgive me, and help me realize the life-and-death seriousness of controlling my tongue. With Your help I will not sin that way again. I receive Your forgiveness now, in Jesus' name. Amen.

James called us to be slow to speak, and that means we should pause and pray before we speak.[12] When we desire change, let's change the way we talk. When we control our tongues, we please the Lord. In his first letter, Peter devoted most of chapter three to relationships and talked about the power of words, saying:

> For
> "He who would love life
> And see good days,
> Let him refrain his tongue from evil,
> And his lips from speaking deceit."
>
> —*1 Peter 3:10*

Sage advice indeed from the man of God.

> *Heavenly Father, help me tame my tongue. Let me speak encouraging words from heaven and not destructive words from hell. Help me pray before I speak. Let me not rattle on when I am stressed or nervous, but hold my peace. Help me maintain control of my tongue when I am afraid, angry, tired, hassled, in pain, frustrated, overwhelmed, and worn out. Help me speak as Jesus would in my situation. Thank you for Your help. In Jesus' name I pray. Amen.*

There is another, often overlooked factor that hinders the power we need in the spiritual conflict. If we resist or rebel against God-constituted authority, our prayers won't work like they should. But when we align ourselves with the Lord's chain of command, His light and grace flow into our lives. We'll learn more about this in the next chapter.

SECRET #15: Learn to control your tongue. A tongue that encourages and builds up people, that speaks life, love, grace, forgiveness, and comfort will be blessed.

---

[12] James 1:19

CHAPTER SIXTEEN

The Covering of Your Local Church

Then the Lord will create above every dwelling place of Mount Zion, and above her assemblies, a cloud and smoke by day and the shining of a flaming fire by night. For over all the glory there will be a covering. —Isaiah 4:5

Have you ever walked somewhere and needed an umbrella? The weatherman predicted light, scattered showers, but now it's coming down like a deluge. Your hair is plastered to your head, and you're not there yet. Owning an umbrella is good, but having it with you when it's raining is better.

The local church is your umbrella

Before Jesus birthed the Church, He declared,

> "And I also say to you that you are Peter [*petros,* a detached stone or boulder], and on this rock [*petra,* a mass of rock] I will build My church, and the gates of Hades shall not prevail against it."
>
> —*Matthew 16:18*

The gates of Hades (hell) cannot prevail against the Church built on Jesus Christ because God's power and protection are present when believers assemble in His name.

But you've probably heard people say, "Well, I don't believe in the organized church." I certainly do for two good reasons! One, my Lord organized it. If it's good enough for Jesus, it's good enough for me. Two, I don't want the enemy oppressing me because I have separated myself from the one institution against which the gates of hell cannot prevail.

Right before Jesus said this, Peter had confessed, "You are the Christ, the Son of the living God!"[1] The Church is the assembly of those who believe what Peter said, whose lives are built on that solid confession. The gates of hell are not able to prevail against the Church's position as the bride of Christ, sharing His authority that comes from God's right hand.

WINDOW IN HEAVEN

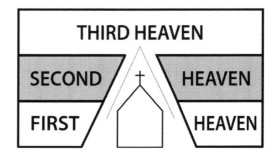

The "open heaven" or "window in heaven" over a worshiping church.

Protection with assembled believers

When I'm going through something, I need to be among believers who are immersed in worship of the living God. The Bible says the Lord *inhabits,* or *is enthroned upon,* the praises of His people.[2] His tangible presence draws near when the Church comes together to praise Him. Angels assemble with believers, helping create a holy atmosphere.

God opens windows in heaven over local churches as they corporately worship in spirit and truth. As the vapors of praise arise, a spiritual cloud forms, and He responds by soaking His people with the rain of His Spirit. The Lord's presence is our shield and covering.

---

[1]   Matthew 16:16

[2]   Psalm 22:3

Then the LORD will create above every dwelling place of Mount Zion, and above her *assemblies*, a cloud and smoke by day and the shining of a flaming fire by night. For over all the glory there will be a *covering*. And there will be a *tabernacle* for shade in the daytime from the heat, for a place of refuge, and for a shelter from storm and rain.

—*Isaiah 4:5–6 (italics added)*

This covering is a protective canopy or defense. It's a "private chamber" into which the people of God can run. It's a shade by day, a fire by night, a place of refuge, and a shelter from the storm. When Israel was trapped at the Red Sea, the pillar of fire moved from in front of them to a position at the rear, between them and the army of Egypt.[3] In the same way, the Lord protects those assembled in His church.

As ideal as this sounds, belonging to a church composed of real people is both rewarding and challenging. The more involved you become, the more you must mesh with other individuals. Some are mature and easy to get along with; some are not. But the overarching promise of church life is this: *the power of the whole is greater than the sum of its individual parts.* We can do more together than we can do apart. It's good for us to belong to something bigger than ourselves, where the goal is saving the world, not just meeting our needs.

Running with the Shepherd

In his insightful book on Christian unity, *Shoulder to Shoulder*, my pastor, Steve Grandy, tells of a vision he had:

> As a young Christian, I struggled with going to church. I seemed to backslide around football season. I had one of those attitudes, "I don't need to be in church. I've been a Christian for two years now. I'm a spiritual giant."
>
> Some of you know what I mean. You have overcoming power and authority in your life…except when football season comes around. My wife Sandy and our three girls would go to church on Sunday, but I'd watch the games.

---

3 Exodus 14:19–20

One night, God dealt with me in a dream. He showed me a flock of sheep and a shepherd walking with them. They had been watered that morning and were passing through green pastures.

As they crossed a large field of open grass, wolves attacked the flock suddenly. I didn't understand what this meant until I noticed something very interesting. The wolves devoured only those that fell behind and those breaking off by themselves to run in their own direction.

The other thing I noticed was that those in the middle of the flock were safe. There was safety in the unity of the flock running together under the care of the shepherd.

Believe me, I never had a problem going to church after that. Some Christians are devoured today because they break off by themselves to do their own little thing, leaving the spiritual safety of God's flock.[4]

We are safe when we abide under the care of the great Shepherd.

Is there an angel of the church?

There was a mighty, protective Angel who accompanied the congregation of Israel in the wilderness.[5] I think local churches also have the protective covering of an angel or company of angels. In Revelation, Jesus tells John to write to the "angels" of the seven churches.[6] This refers to the pastors as the "messengers" of God in each church, but I don't overlook the fact that angels were assigned to those churches when they were planted, like God assigned to the congregation of Israel.

For example, Steve Grandy was sent by God to Paradise, California, to plant a church. I have no doubt that God sent at least one powerful angel to help him and his family with that assignment, and that angel still covers and protects the entire church body.

As Christians, we often take local churches for granted and discount them as common things. Churches are *uncommon*. They represent the

---

[4] Steve Grandy, *Shoulder to Shoulder* (Paradise, CA: Jubilee On The Ridge, 1993), pp. 104–105. Used by permission.

[5] Exodus 23:20–22

[6] Revelation 2:1, 8, 12, etc.

calling of God upon faithful and dedicated individuals who sacrificed to pray, listen, obey, and plant a church where the Lord sent them.

> *When I'm going through something, I need to be in an assembly of believers immersed in worship of the living God. The Bible says the Lord inhabits, or is enthroned upon, the praises of His people.*

When we join a church, we come under the protective umbrella and authority of that founding pastor, the angels God sent with him or her, the organization that appointed them (if any), and those pastors who have followed. We are connected with the prayers of all the intercessors who have prayed mightily for that church. When you think about it like this, churches are indeed unique and special.

The church is like a military organization

A Roman centurion came to Jesus, and he understood things about His ministry we often miss. Jesus marveled and then commended this man's "great faith."[7] The centurion understood Jesus as the "General" over a heavenly army. This military man understood how authority worked, and it gave him great faith. He knew all Jesus had to do was issue an order—to "speak the Word"—and all heaven would obey.

The centurion understood the principles of submission and authority. If he submitted to the leaders *over* him, he had authority over those *under* him. If he rebelled against those over him, he would be stripped of his authority over those under him.

All authority in the church world flows down from Jesus in designated channels. Local church members need to submit to the authority of their pastors in spiritual things. When we maintain a right relationship to those over us, our personal spiritual authority operates over things under us, such as the spiritual forces in the second heaven. Then God's angelic covering protects us.

---

[7] Matthew 8:5–10

Don't grieve your shepherd.

> Obey those who rule over you, and be submissive, for they watch
> out for your souls, as those who must give account. Let them do so with
> joy and not with grief, for that would be *unprofitable for you.*
> —*Hebrews 13:17 (italics added)*

When we submit to our leaders, we can "speak the Word" with power, and heaven backs us up, including the angel of the church. But if we refuse to submit to those over us, the flow from above is hindered. Our words and prayers have diminished authority and fruitfulness.

The *office* of pastor is ordained by God.[8] While it's true that imperfect men occupy the office, we are to submit to them out of respect for God. If the person in the office abuses their authority, God will correct or remove them. But if our issue with the leader is relatively minor, like the color of new carpet, the method used to achieve a common goal, or a difference in leadership style, we do well not to speak against the authority.

Can pastors be wrong sometimes? Absolutely. Like the rest of us they need prayer and good counsel. If the situation warrants it, we may prayerfully, tactfully, and lovingly share our wisdom with him or her. But if nothing comes from that, we are well-advised to hold our peace and remain submitted for the sake of our protection and covering. (Be aware that decisions your pastor makes may be based on information not known to you. Because of confidentiality, pastors know more than they can reveal.)

Scripture warns, "Do not touch My anointed ones, and do My prophets no harm."[9] Miriam and Aaron spoke against Moses, and God rebuked them.[10] Korah and others rose up against Moses and Aaron and were destroyed.[11] When individuals rebelled against Paul and persisted in heresy, God lifted His protection.[12] These are examples to us, and not for the purpose of making a pastor a dictator, but that we may not hinder the flow of authority so necessary for us to fight well spiritually.

---

[8] Ephesians 4:11
[9] Psalm 105:15
[10] Numbers 12:1–16
[11] Numbers 16
[12] 1 Timothy 1:20

Local churches and pastors are gifts from God to provide a covering in the locality where we are. "Lone Ranger" Christians miss so much. (A "Lone Ranger" Christian is one who is not planted in a local church, usually because of an unresolved offense that occurred in a previous church.) Let's forgive whoever offended us in days past and move on. See the bigger picture, join, get involved, and pay tithes where you are covered. As you respect the office and speak well of those in authority over you, God covers you with His umbrella of protection like a shield.

> Those who are *planted* in the house of the LORD
> Shall flourish in the courts of our God.
> —*Psalm 92:13 (italics added)*

If the "rain" of circumstances is getting you wet and it seems you have no "umbrella," ask yourself: "Am I in a right relationship with my pastor and the fellow members of my church? Am I causing division within the body or walking in love toward all?" Division breaks down the unity necessary for the proper functioning of the whole. Can you imagine the mess you would be in if your left leg refused to cooperate with your right leg? You wouldn't be able to walk.

Jesus said that a house divided against itself cannot stand.[13] Unity is necessary in a congregation for the Spirit to flow. Division and friction quench the Spirit, but walking in love and unity releases it. King David in the Psalms wrote this: "Behold, how good and how pleasant it is for brethren to dwell together in unity!"[14] Not only is it pleasant, it is protected.

> *Heavenly Father, thank You for the angels and protection You provide through my local church. Help me show respect for my pastor and his God-called office. As I honor him, I honor You and bring my family and myself under the protective covering of the church. I will strive to keep the unity of the Spirit in the bond of peace. In Jesus' name I pray. Amen.*

---

[13] Matthew 12:25
[14] Psalm 133:1

Don't ignore tithing

About a thousand years after the law of Moses was given, God told the prophet Malachi that if God's people brought their tithes into the local storehouse (the church), He would open windows in heaven over them and pour out such a blessing they would not have room to receive it.[15] He also promised to *rebuke the devourer* for their sakes so that they could be a blessed people. The devourer is that which consumes and destroys investments and belongings, causing loss.

In the last book of the Old Testament, only four hundred years before Christ, God was still communicating the importance of tithing. Why would He do this if it was soon to pass away? Honoring God with our tithes releases His blessing in a way nothing else does. The best way to apply protection over your belongings is to pay your tithes, because that is the only way to have God rebuke the devourer in your life. To live in the light, we have to be doers of the Word.

Bringing tithes to your local church honors Jesus Christ. Under the Old Testament, men paid tithes to mortal priests who died. How much more should we be eager to bring our tithes (in care of our local church) to Jesus, our great High Priest who lives forever![16]

So far, we have discussed the core principles of spiritual warfare and protection. In the next chapter we'll talk about how to keep a balanced perspective about living in both a material and spiritual world.

SECRET #16: Do not forsake going to church, for it provides a spiritual covering against which the gates of hell cannot prevail. Submit to the spiritual authority over you and refrain from causing division, a sin that weakens the body of Christ.

---

[15] Malachi 3:8–12

[16] Hebrews 7

CHAPTER SEVENTEEN

A Balanced View of
Spiritual Warfare

Blessed be the LORD my Rock,
Who trains my hands for war,
And my fingers for battle—
—Psalm 144:1

I t's one thing to know about spiritual warfare and another to handle the knowledge wisely. People often go to extremes. Some ignore the spiritual realm as though it did not exist, but Jesus did not do this. On the other hand, some are so obsessed with the spirit world they're casting evil spirits out of everything. Jesus did not do that either. So what should our strategy be?

We have to recognize when we are under attack

Everyone has a "normal" range of emotions and attitudes, but sometimes we or a person close to us starts acting in a way outside their normal. They may get touchy or cranky. Of course, they could be hungry, not getting enough sleep, have a headache, or otherwise be in pain. But if those things are not the issue, such symptoms can be a sign of spiritual warfare, or a sign they are under conviction from the Holy Spirit because they need to change something in their life.

Here's a short list of symptoms that may indicate we're dealing with spiritual challenges: irritability, lack of patience, stress, lack of energy, tight mental pressure (like your mind is being squeezed in a vise), sleeplessness, inability to think clearly, depression, dullness, lack of creativity, trouble recalling God's Word, difficulty praying, lack of desire to go to church, unforgiveness, and feeling like your old sins are coming back. (Some of these can be symptoms of physical issues, too.)

When things go beyond normal, your first reaction will probably be, *What did I do wrong now?* But it might not be you at all. A spiritual attack may be trying to stop your spiritual growth or hinder your godly influence. Jesus said, "Blessed are those who are persecuted for *righteousness'* sake, for theirs is the kingdom of heaven."[1] When we do right, we may face opposition or backlash. So if things are going sideways, you may have to ask yourself, *What did I do right now?*

How do we deal with spiritual warfare?

Here are some things we can do to fight back:

- Stop arguing and pray with your spouse. Don't discuss sensitive topics when the spiritual atmosphere is explosive.

- Pray with your pastor, group leader, or prayer partner.

- Plead the blood of Jesus to affirm your right standing.

- Apply the blood of Jesus to your "house" (your person and your dwelling) to remind the spirit world you are under the Passover protection.

- Command your mountain to move in Jesus' name.

- Put your trust in the promises of God.

- Fast and pray.

- Fellowship with encouraging Christians.

- Speak positive and stay upbeat. This too shall pass.

- Increase your Bible reading and devotional time.

- Listen to Christian music or watch Christian television.

- Sing to the Lord. It changes the atmosphere around you.

- Pray often in your prayer language.

---

[1]   Matthew 5:10

- Regularly attend an alive church that gives you a spiritual boost. Go more than once a week. Join a small group or Bible study that will encourage and pray with you.

- Force yourself to do constructive things in your spare time— straighten the house, wash clothes, clean the garage, work on your hobby, or go for a drive to break the grip of the status quo. Refuse to isolate yourself, and don't let the enemy trap you in your house like a bird in a cage.

Don't be discouraged if the pressure does not lift immediately. Some battles take longer than others. If you are driving a heavy truck up a hill, you shift to a lower gear. Your speed will drop, but you'll have more power to make the grade. We need to "downshift" in times of spiritual warfare. This may be frustrating at first because things are taking longer than we thought, but tap into the strength of God and wear the enemy out. The Bible says, "Therefore submit to God. Resist the devil and he will flee from you."[2] "He who is in you is greater than he who is in the world."[3]

Answers to prayer hindered in the second heaven

Answers to prayer can be delayed by warfare in the second heaven. After twenty-one days of prayer and fasting, the prophet Daniel was encouraged by a glorious, heavenly messenger.

> Then he said to me, "Do not fear, Daniel, for from the first day that you set your heart to understand, and to humble yourself before your God, your words were heard; and I have come because of your words. *But the prince of the kingdom of Persia withstood me twenty-one days;* and behold, Michael, one of the chief princes, came to help me, for I had been left alone there with the kings of Persia."
> —*Daniel 10:12–13 (italics added)*

The messenger, perhaps the angel Gabriel, was dispatched from God's throne in the third heaven to encourage Daniel, but he needed assistance to fight through the second heaven to deliver the message. The warring angel Michael came to help him. (Michael still invisibly

---

[2] James 4:7

[3] 1 John 4:4

defends, fights for, and protects Israel.) If your prayers are not answered right away, don't give up. The answer is on the way, but there's a battle going on in the second heaven. Keep believing with persistent faith, and your answer will break through. Perseverance always pays off.

Finding the balance

So how do we fight spiritual warfare? Is it all about standing up in our authority in Christ and rebuking the darkness, or is there more to it than that? Two main thoughts have helped me here.

First, the Lord won a great victory and gave us authority to rebuke the devil emphatically. We can command our mountains to be removed in His name. We are to put on the full armor of God and resist the devil.

Answers to prayers can be delayed by warfare in the second heaven.

Second, our focus must remain the *kingdom* of heaven, not the devil or the second heaven. Paul made this point when he said,

> If then you were raised with Christ, *seek those things which are above, where Christ is, sitting at the right hand of God.* Set your mind on *things above,* not on things on the earth.
> —*Colossians 3:1–2 (italics added)*

A story is told of a man who set out on a quest for treasure and was sidetracked by glittering trinkets. He never discovered the real thing. People often miss the main event because of sideshows and counterfeits. Yes, the second heaven is out there, calling through "new age" and occult teachings, but Jesus is the real treasure. He is loving and life-giving, higher, kinder, and better than any sideshow. So never be more fascinated with the spirit world than you are with Jesus. Remember the example of Peter. He walked on water *as long as he kept his eyes on Jesus.*

Lighting a candle or cursing the darkness?

Darkness is always dispelled by light. *It's more effective to light a candle than to curse the darkness.* This concept changed my life. Obsessing about darkness is not as helpful as lighting a candle.

But what candle do we light? Proverbs 20:27 tells us, *"The spirit of a man is the lamp [candle] of the Lord."* Our spirit, the part of us that contacts God, is a built-in lamp or candle. When our spirit shines with the glory of God, it radiates light that displaces darkness. Effective spiritual warfare is worshiping and meditating on the Lord, who is light.[4]

It's more effective to light a candle than to curse the darkness.

So when things are dark, stand up to the devil, use your authority, rebuke him sharply, but don't camp there. Turn your focus to the Lord. Light your candle! Sing praises to the Lord. Read the Word of God. Go to an "alive" church service. Listen to Christian music and Bible teachings that encourage and build you up. Darkness and depression flee when your inner man burns with the light of Christ. For this reason, Paul admonished believers to stay filled with the Holy Spirit, singing, praising, and thanking the Lord.[5] As you focus on Him, who is light, you remain full of light, and the darkness cannot penetrate.

> *Heavenly Father, help me recognize when my family and I are under attack. Give us the strength we need to fight back with spiritual weapons. Help us light our candles and repel the darkness by keeping our eyes on You. In Jesus' name, I pray. Amen.*

We are to submit to God and resist the devil, and the next chapter will help us know what to resist.

SECRET #17: Recognize when you are under attack and downshift into warfare mode. Don't isolate yourself but spend more time with God and His people. Keep your eyes on Jesus and your spirit burning with His Word and Holy Spirit.

---

[4] John 8:12, 1 Timothy 6:16, Matthew 17:2, 1 John 1:5
[5] Ephesians 5:18–21

CHAPTER EIGHTEEN

Is It God or the Devil?

"Resist him, steadfast in the faith..." —1 Peter 5:9

Jesus won the ultimate victory over the enemy, but He could not remove all evil from the earth because mankind still had the right to choose. If every man, woman, and child refused the evil and chose the good, evil would be overcome in one glorious day. But until that happens, both good and evil are present, and we can't change that reality.

Resist the devil!

The apostles described the proper attitude toward evil.

> *Therefore submit to God. Resist the devil and he will flee from you.*
> —*James 4:7 (italics added)*

> Be sober, be vigilant; because your adversary the devil walks about like a roaring lion, seeking whom he *may* devour. *Resist him, steadfast in the faith,* knowing that the same sufferings are experienced by your brotherhood in the world.
> —*1 Peter 5:8–9 (italics added)*

> Put on the whole armor of God, that *you may be able to stand against the wiles of the devil.*
> —*Ephesians 6:11 (italics added)*

Living a life in submission to God is the first step in resisting. Close the open doors (ungodly behaviors, addictions, and practices) that allow the enemy free entry into your soul. Submitted Christians get results when they resist. But if we have open doors in our lives, we chase the devil out one door, and he tiptoes back in another.

Peter said the devil walks about *like* a roaring lion, but he isn't a roaring lion because the Lord pulled his teeth 2,000 years ago. The Alpha Lion in the spirit realm is Jesus—the "Lion of the tribe of Judah"![1] Peter said the devil seeks someone he *may* devour. "May" is a word of permission. You have dominion, so don't give him permission to devour you or your family. The only ones devoured are the ones who don't resist.

> *John 10:10 is the dividing line of spiritual discernment. On one side is the life-giving hand of the Good Shepherd, and on the other the death-dealing hand of the thief.*

Recently, a mountain lion was sighted in a local park here in northern California. A young lady and her dog were walking on a trail when the lion approached. Her dog took a stand courageously between her and the lion. The young lady escaped, but her dog gave his life. On the evening news, park rangers issued the following instructions. If you see a lion, make yourself appear as large as you can and back away slowly. If attacked, *fight back!* This is good advice for fighting the devil, other than the backing up part. *We are to live large in Christ and fight him with everything we have.*

If you were the devil, who would you attack? Someone who always resists you, calling on the name of Jesus? Or somebody who doesn't know you are there, isn't watchful, and won't fight back? When we keep resisting, he'll leave us for easier prey. Never give up. Wear the devil out in the strength of Jesus. He will flee from *you!*

Temptations of the flesh

We begin resisting by controlling our flesh. Urges to indulge fleshly appetites are easy to recognize. The human body is neutral, being

---

[1]   Revelation 5:5

neither good nor bad, but it can be used as a vessel for honor or dis-
honor. When fleshly appetites become compulsions, especially when we
can't control them, a stronghold is at the root of the problem. It must be
attacked with the Word of God and prayer. Volume 2 of this series, *Tearing Down Strongholds,* will help you overcome the flesh and win the
battle in your mind. When we walk in the Spirit, we do not fulfill the
lusts of the flesh. Instead, we crucify them.[2]

Discerning the hand of God from the hand of the devil

Jesus fought with more than the temptations of the flesh. He over-
came demons, sickness, and forces of nature, as well as attitudes like
pride, greed, and lust for power. We're on solid ground whenever we
resist what He opposed. He came against ignorance and spiritual darkness by His teaching and preaching. He came against disease, infirmity,
and demons through His healing ministry.

By observing what He fought against in the Gospels, we clearly see
what is of God and what is of the devil. As our Master Teacher, Jesus
taught a plain lesson on how to discern good from evil. He made it simple so all can understand it.

> "The *thief* does not come except *to steal, and to kill, and to destroy. I
> have come that they may have life, and that they may have it more abun-
> dantly.* I am the good shepherd. The good shepherd gives His life for the
> sheep."
>
> *—John 10:10–11 (italics added)*

The "sheep" (people) belong to God. The thief (the devil) comes to
steal, kill, and destroy them. Loss, sickness, death, accidents, and
destruction are the work of the thief coming to steal our finances, rob
our health, crush our spirits, kill our families, and destroy our lives. But
Jesus came that His sheep may have an abundant, overcoming, and
blessed life. The Bible says, "For this purpose the Son of God was manifested, that He might destroy the works of the devil."[3]

---

[2]   Galatians 5:16–24
[3]   1 John 3:8

John 10:10 is the dividing line of spiritual discernment. On one side is the life-giving hand of the Good Shepherd and on the other the death-dealing hand of the thief. If it's good, it's from God.[4] If it's bad, it's from the devil. This is not difficult, so we don't have to be deceived. God is a good God, and the devil is a bad devil.

This sounds overly simple, but many sincere believers think God permits the devil to attack them in order to teach them spiritual lessons.[5] If that's the case, I'm confused. How can I resist a stealing, killing, or destroying circumstance if it's being *allowed* by God? Would I not be resisting God's will? And who am I to fight against Him? In other words, if God put sickness on me to teach me something, going to the doctor would be resisting His will. How do we make sense of this?

Jesus is our chief theologian and final interpreter of Scripture. He knew God and His ways better than anyone, and we don't see anywhere in the Gospels where Jesus gave demons permission to attack God's children. Jesus never made deals with demons—He cast them out. He made war against them. He came to destroy them. He said, "He who has seen Me has seen the Father."[6] It was Adam and Eve who gave the devil permission to attack the human race, not the Father or Jesus.

To God, the end never justifies the means

Personally, I don't believe God uses the devil to spank His kids any more than you would hire a gangster to teach your child a lesson. Our righteous Father loves righteousness and hates iniquity.[7] He will not use the instigator of all that is evil to correct His children—even to achieve an alleged good. If a human made a deal with the devil to teach the people around him a lesson, he would be guilty of witchcraft. God hates witchcraft, so why would He practice it himself?

To God, the end never justifies the means. A righteous God uses righteous means to accomplish righteous purposes. Otherwise, the unrighteous means contaminate the end result. According to the law of

---

[4]   James 1:17
[5]   As discussed in Chapter Six, "Standing Taller than Fallen Angels," the events of Job 1–2 cannot be repeated and do not apply to Christians.
[6]   John 14:9
[7]   Psalm 11:7, 5:5, 45:7

sowing and reaping,[8] what a person sows (the means) determines what he reaps (the end).

God would never use an unrighteous devil to achieve righteous purposes. That would be like performing heart surgery with a rusty, unsterilized scalpel, expecting the patient not to get infected. It would be like washing white clothes in muddy water or wiping your kitchen counter with a rag you just used to clean the toilet. Yuck!

Demons are called "unclean spirits" for a reason, and the devil is the dirtiest of them all, being the embodiment of all spiritual and moral filth. So how could God use the "great contaminator" to make His people clean? But suppose, for the sake of argument, He "allowed" the devil to afflict a person to teach him patience. Suppose he learned a little patience but in the presence of uncleanness became addicted to pornography. (An unclean spirit transmits its uncleanness.) Was the individual helped? Not really. For this reason, God corrects His children with the righteous means of His Word and Holy Spirit.

Personally, I don't believe God uses the devil to spank His kids any more than you would hire a gangster to teach your child a lesson.

The "chastening of the Lord" described in Scripture is not the *circumstance* of trouble, but the *conviction* the Word and Holy Spirit bring when we do not handle the circumstance in faith, patience, and love. We are not to despise the chastening of the Lord, nor be discouraged when we are *rebuked* by Him.[9] *God's Word* is His agent of correction, not circumstances,[10] and for this reason the Word is called the rod of God.[11] Adam and Eve *allowed* enough evil into the world to teach every man and woman great patience and faith without God lifting a finger.

---

8   Galatians 6:7–8
9   Hebrews 12:5, John 16:7–8
10   2 Timothy 3:16–17
11   Micah 6:9

Jesus stated that *all* authority had been given to Him in heaven and on earth.[12] If all authority belongs to Jesus, then the enemy is running around with no authority. Having no authority means that God has *not authorized* him to afflict anyone in order to teach them a lesson. The devil has no sanction or permission from God to do anything. He is in rebellion against the authority of God, refuses to submit to God's righteous rule, and cannot be trusted with the least amount of authority.

The devil's favorite trap

The devil delights in afflicting the people of God and then telling them that God did it to them or "allowed" it. *Don't fall into the trap of blaming God for what the devil did!* God is good, and the devil is bad. When bad things come, it's from the devil, whom we are to resist until he flees from us.

What about sickness?

Personally, I've grown greatly in patience and faith during tough times by learning to trust God, but the Lord did not send the tough times to teach me those lessons. He didn't have to because the evil was already in the world. When the Lord gave Adam free will, He determined to permit whatever Adam and his children (us) would permit. Trouble, sickness, and the devil have been in the world since Adam and Eve desired the knowledge of evil and sanctioned its presence by eating the fruit of disobedience.

Suppose I'm living a lukewarm Christian life and spend more time fishing on Sunday than in church. But one day I receive a bad report from the doctor. Now I want to call on God for healing but am ashamed to ask Him after neglecting church. Let's assume I repent, change my ways, and go back to church regularly. Did God *send* the sickness to correct me? No. Sickness was already in the world. Did God guide me back to Himself through the sickness for my good? Absolutely.

Sickness is not the hand of God, but He can make all things work together for our good. Sickness is a thief coming to steal our health, finances, and harm our families. But if we think sickness is the hand of

---

[12] Matthew 28:18

God, we may passively pray, "If the Lord wills, may I recover." But if we discern it as a *thief* coming to steal our health, we resist it aggressively with every tool at our disposal, including faith, prayer, and medicine. Doctors acknowledge that the attitude of the patient has a lot to do with their outcome. Believers and fighters survive.

Jesus treated sickness as an enemy, the product of the Fall. He went about doing good and healing all who were oppressed by the devil.[13] For this reason, we should resist sickness like He did and call upon the Lord for His healing power to manifest in our bodies. By His stripes He purchased healing for us two thousand years ago.[14] Don't be shy about appropriating what belongs to you. Don't be afraid to use your faith in God's Word along with modern medicine and other practical wisdom, such as diet and exercise.

If we fight serious illness and don't win that battle, we have done well by fighting the good fight of faith and will inherit an eternal reward. Plus, we leave an example of determination for others. We are all going to die sometime, but when we go out in faith and courage, we win!

What about cancer?

Never ask why God put cancer on this person or that person, because God doesn't put cancer on anyone. Where would He get it? There's no cancer in heaven. When did Jesus ever put a disease on anyone? Cancer is not a work of God but of the thief coming to steal someone. Cancer is the operation of the law of sin and death that came from the Fall. Blaming God for it is ignorance.

In Christ is life and healing to overcome cancer. When we get well, we rejoice. If we don't make it, our life was extended by faith and prayer, and we depart with grace and dignity in the embrace of the Holy Spirit. The Bible says, "For the law of the Spirit of life in Christ Jesus has made me free from the law of sin and death."[15] People die from the working of the "law of sin and death." People live because the more powerful "law of the Spirit of life" sets them free. We will not live forever in this fallen world, but while we are here we have the blessing of the Spirit of life

---

[13] Acts 10:38, Luke 13:15–16, Matthew 9:35
[14] Isaiah 53:4–5
[15] Romans 8:2

operating in our bodies to overcome sin and death that we may finish the work He has given us to do.

Jesus rebuked the forces of nature

Jesus also rebuked the wind and waves that threatened to swamp the boat as He and the disciples crossed the Sea of Galilee. If the windstorm was an "act of God" (as insurance companies call such things), then Jesus successfully rebuked God! But if the storm was a simple act of nature or a demonic attack, then He demonstrated authority over the forces of nature, which authority He transferred to the Church.[16] We can use our authority in His name against tornadoes, typhoons, hurricanes, high seas, and tsunamis, and command them to dissipate and be still.

Don't be confused. Discern the hand of God from the hand of evil. Resist the devil. Put up a fight, and he will flee from you. As we dwell in the light, the darkness is exposed with its deception and lies.

> *Father, may I always resist evil in Your might. I can do all things through Christ who strengthens me. I call on the Spirit of life from God to replace infirmity and death in my body with health. I resist bad attitudes, evil words, evil thoughts, addictions, and immorality, and set my heart to believe You for the best in all things. As I resist, I renew my mind to the things of God and acquire the mind of Christ. When I believe right, I will live right. Thank You for strengthening me, in Jesus' name. Amen.*

No discussion of spiritual warfare is complete without learning how to put on the armor of light, which is the armor of God. The next chapter will strengthen you to fight your battles!

SECRET #18: Submit to God and resist the devil in every way he comes against you. Don't simply endure evil but resist it until it flees from you in terror! Don't blame God for the works of the thief. He is not your problem, but your ally and Savior in times of trouble.

---

[16] Matthew 28:18

CHAPTER NINETEEN

How to Really Put On the Armor of Light

The night is far spent, the day is at hand. Therefore let us cast off the works of darkness, and let us put on the armor of light.
—Romans 13:12

Suppose your enemy sees a tall, good-looking warrior advancing toward him. This soldier is wearing impressive armor with a highly polished breastplate gleaming in the sunlight. He is the picture of strength with huge pecs and washboard abs. He is vigilant—attentive, on guard, and searching for the adversary. His mind is focused, and his sword sharp and drawn. When the enemy sees him, he recognizes the armor because it looks like *God's armor!* He does not dare attack someone who looks like God because it might be God, so he slinks away.

When I think of strapping on the intimidating armor of God, my attitude is energized. I stand tall and stick my chest out, becoming militant, thinking strategically, confident in who I am. But I've also had days when I didn't feel so confident, when I was overwhelmed by the pressures of life, when the darkness in the room seemed so thick I could carve my initials in it. Where was my armor in those hours? Had I forgotten to put it on? Or did I have it on but needed to oil and polish it properly? What was I missing?

Having experienced highs and lows in spiritual warfare while maintaining a consistent Christian lifestyle, I've found myself asking a tough but necessary question: *How do I really put on the armor of God, and how does it work?*

If we let the Word of God settle every question, and we should, then we need to find out what the Bible has to say about spiritual armor. The first reference to armor in Scripture was God's promise to Abraham: *"I am your shield,"*[1] which we've discussed at length. The prophet Isaiah described the Redeemer of Israel wearing a breastplate and a helmet.[2]

Armor is briefly mentioned in Psalm 91:4: *"His truth shall be your shield and buckler."* That short phrase contains an awesome insight: *God's truth functions in our lives like armor.* Based on this verse alone we could call the armor of God the "armor of truth." We know that the entrance of God's truth (Word) gives light in the inner man,[3] so it's not much of a stretch to see how the apostle Paul might call the "armor of truth" the "armor of light."

> The night is far spent, the day is at hand. Therefore let us cast off the works of darkness, *and let us put on the armor of light.*
> —*Romans 13:12 (italics added)*

Could we conclude that the armor of God has something to do with the "light" and "truth" that come from God's Word? If so, then understanding the truths of the Gospel will armor us to withstand all opposition.

Before we draw conclusions, the New Testament has a great deal more to say. The book of Ephesians contains the Bible's most detailed treatment of the armor. Since the apostle Paul was the most criticized and persecuted preacher of his day, he was well qualified to teach on this subject. While a prisoner of Rome, he was guarded by and chained to Roman soldiers and was familiar with their equipment as well.

The Roman army was the best-equipped fighting force in the ancient world, owing much of its success to the superiority of its armor. Paul knew every part of the soldier's equipment and compared the armor of God to Roman armor. Before we analyze each piece and how it protects us, it's important to notice the way Paul introduces the subject.

---

[1]   Genesis 15:1

[2]   Isaiah 59:16–17

[3]   Psalm 119:130, Ephesians 1:17–18

Finally, my brethren, be strong in the Lord and in the power of His might. Put on the whole armor of God, that you may be able to stand against the wiles of the devil. For we do not wrestle against flesh and blood, but against principalities, against powers, against the rulers of the darkness of this age, against spiritual hosts of wickedness in the heavenly places. Therefore take up the whole armor of God, that you may be able to withstand in the evil day, and having done all, to stand.

—Ephesians 6:10–13

First, be *"strong in the Lord."* Jesus defeated the devil decisively when He went to the cross and rose from the dead. In His strength we are strong, not in our own strength. He is the Vine and we are the branches.[4] We are to abide in Him, drawing strength and nourishment from Him. We are to walk, talk, and think in Christ.

Next, we are to "put on" the whole armor of God. Who must put it on? We must! God supplies the armor, but we are the ones who put it on. We need to put on the "whole armor," including every piece. Half the armor only half protects us.

Paul talked about the battle we face and who the real enemy is. Though it seems our battle is against flesh and blood, we are not striving against the *people* who oppose us. We wrestle against "principalities and powers," against spiritual forces in the second heaven we cannot see, who use and manipulate the people we can see. In Christ, we have the ability to exercise authority over these forces, so the people controlled by them may be freed to make better choices.

We need God's armor so we will be able to "withstand" evil and remain standing on the field. An excellent definition of "withstand" is found in the *New Spirit Filled Life Bible:* "vigorously opposing, bravely resisting, standing face-to-face against an adversary, standing your ground."[5] When the conflict is over, we will be found standing victoriously on the field.

---

[4]   John 15:1–5
[5]   Dick Mills, "Word Wealth," *New Spirit-Filled Life Bible,* ed. Jack W. Hayford (Nashville, TN: Thomas Nelson, Inc., 2002), p. 1654.

Exactly what is the armor of God?

> Stand therefore, having girded your waist with *truth,* having put on the breastplate of *righteousness,* and having shod your feet with the *preparation* of the gospel of peace; above all, taking the shield of *faith* with which you will be able to quench all the fiery darts of the wicked one. And take the helmet of *salvation,* and the sword of the Spirit, which is the *word of God; praying always* with all prayer and supplication in the Spirit, being watchful to this end with all perseverance and supplication for all the saints.
>
> —*Ephesians 6:14–18 (italics added)*

Every pastor or Bible teacher addresses the armor of God at one time or another. It's a fascinating subject, and I love hearing various points of view on what each piece of the armor does. Here, of course, I'm presenting my view which has developed over time. Perhaps it differs slightly from what you have heard before, but that's okay. *In a multitude of counselors there is safety.*[6] Learn what you can from each one, and above all put on each piece of the armor and use it as best you understand it.

When I first heard about the armor of God, I was excited. At last, here was something to help me deal with the warfare I endured. My mind was constantly bombarded with thoughts reminding me of my past failures, and I secretly felt like Paul, chief among sinners.

One day on Christian radio, I heard a preacher coach a congregation through the motions of putting on the armor of God. He had everyone stand to their feet. I stood up at home. He instructed everyone to wrap a girdle around their waist. I tightened an invisible girdle around myself. We put on the breastplate and buckled it tight. We strapped on battle sandals and stomped our feet vigorously to let the devil know he was under our feet. We took up the shield of faith, put the helmet of salvation over our head and buckled it. Very carefully we drew the super-sharp sword of the Spirit out of its scabbard, brandishing it in every direction and declaring "It is written!" like Jesus did.

---

[6]   Proverbs 11:14, 24:6

It was fun and energized my faith. Every day I repeated these motions with a militant attitude and visualized spiritual objects like armor being put on my body. I was confident I had the armor figured out although I wasn't sure if I had to do this every day or not. I noticed that the days I did were better days, for such an exercise stirred up my faith. But after the newness wore off, I would forget to "put on the armor."

Armor as a series of "revelations"?

A few years later, I heard another preacher declare that we put on the armor when we receive the "revelation" of each piece. This messed up my thinking. I was all ears to learn how to do this, but he did not explain. Armor as "revelation"? Armor as "revealed truth"? I could not get his words out of my mind. Revelation of what? How could this work?

My curiosity (actually the Holy Spirit) drove me to read the Ephesians passage over and over. The first piece of armor was the girdle (belt) of truth, so the revelation would have something to do with truth. How could truth act like a girdle? The second piece was the breastplate of righteousness, so the revelation of righteousness would function like a breastplate. As I worked through the pieces of armor, a pattern emerged that began with truth, added an understanding of righteousness, then preparation or readiness, then faith, salvation, the uttered Word, and prayer. As I wrestled with this list, I saw that a clear revelation of each piece would give me victory in a particular area of conflict.

What I learned revolutionized my thinking! The armor of God is not a series of invisible objects dropped on us from heaven. Paul used Roman armor as a *metaphor,* a figure of speech, and an illustration of a spiritual reality. *It's easy to get so caught up studying Roman armor that we miss the point.*

To put on the armor of light Paul talked about, I needed more than a *visualization* of Roman armor, I needed a *revelation* (a God-given understanding) of the following seven things: *truth, righteousness, readiness, faith, the hope of salvation, using the Word as a weapon,* and *prayer.* The armor that protects our souls is what we *believe.* Jesus said it like this, "You shall know the *truth,* and the *truth* shall make you free."[7]

---

[7] John 8:32

Training ourselves in these seven areas protects us from the deceiving thoughts of the enemy. Each successive revelation of truth transforms our thinking from weakness and defeat to triumph and victory. Putting on the armor is real-life discipleship that creates strong and mighty warriors, champions for Christ. *The armor of God is the armor of a renewed mind!*

The Belt of Truth

We gird our waist with truth when we make the quality decision to take the Bible as *our* source of light and standard of truth, cinching it tightly around our lives. When we do so, the Bible, especially the New Testament, becomes our authoritative guide for faith and practice.

> *To "put on" the armor, I needed more than a visualization of Roman armor, I needed a revelation (a God-given understanding) of the following seven things: truth, righteousness, readiness, faith, the hope of salvation, using the Word as a weapon, and prayer.*

To put on the belt of truth, we must accept the whole counsel of God, the parts we like and the parts we don't like. Trusting the Bible to guide our thinking protects us from the darkness of confusion and deception that is in the world.

Think about it: Jesus exposed Satan as a liar and the father of all lies.[8] The enemy has skillfully woven half-truths and outright lies into the culture, so that what is moral and upright is made to appear bad, and what is immoral and bad is made to sound good.

But Jesus said, "I am the way, the truth, and the life."[9] Jesus spoke the truth and nothing but the truth. Truth is our weapon against every lie, so you can see why making an intentional commitment to God's truth is

---

[8] John 8:44

[9] John 14:6

the *first* piece of the armor of God, and all the other pieces depend on it. You can also see why renewing one's mind in God's Word is so important. Either God's Word reprograms us from the world's lies, or we will continue in worldly ways.

Only God's truth, which originates outside of ourselves, can keep us on the right track. Putting humans in charge of truth is about as wise as putting the wolf in charge of the chicken coop. The self-serving desires of the flesh will determine the outcome, as "truth" gets bent in every direction to accommodate a person's whims. To justify our actions, we say, "You have your truth, and I have my truth." But all "truths" are not pure, nor do they produce the same results.

A compass, for example, is a guide that exists outside of ourselves. It is useful in a thick forest where we can't see our way clearly, precisely because it always points north, regardless of which direction I personally think is north. Like a compass, the Word of God is the only guidance system that can keep us on the path of eternal life.

Of all the world's religious teachers, only Jesus was the Son of God, knew the Father intimately, taught about the *kingdom* of heaven, died as a sacrifice to free mankind from sin, and sent the Spirit of Truth into our hearts. God's Word is an external and objective standard that defends us from the "spirit of error" that's in the world.[10] Truth is not defined by what I think, how I feel, what I want, or what someone else wants for me, but by what God says. When I put on the girdle of truth, I have made a firm decision to let the Bible settle every question.

Many people have the belt of truth in their hands or on their nightstand, but they haven't found the courage and faith to wear it. Some have wrapped it loosely around their waist, but it's not tied on where it becomes a part of them. The Bible must become the determining factor in your decision-making process if it is going to protect you.

Of course, when we have girded our waist with truth, we need to be truthful in speech. How can we walk in truth if we don't speak truth? After all, when we speak the truth in love, we push away the father of lies and extricate ourselves from that sticky web of lying that gets us all tangled up, deceiving and being deceived.

---

[10] 1 John 4:6

The Breastplate of Righteousness

The breastplate of a Roman soldier protected his heart and vital organs, and the spiritual breastplate protects our spiritual heart. It seems obvious that the way to put on this breastplate is to do good deeds of righteousness. As a young Christian, I learned that making right decisions repelled the devil and gave him no place in my life. Plus, I experienced joy when I did the right thing. When I obeyed God, my heart was protected, and I lived free from guilt, condemnation, and the messy consequences of sin.

But some days I did or said the wrong thing, and my conscience condemned me. The fiery arrows of guilt penetrated my core, and I felt unworthy and ashamed to pray. When I needed God most, I was separated from His help. My communication line (of prayer) to my Commander in Chief was cut in the middle of the attack, and I couldn't call in reinforcements. My spiritual heart lay bleeding and exposed to the enemy. Where was my breastplate when I needed it? Did it fall off when I did wrong? Though I constantly confessed my sins to God, I rarely felt accepted and forgiven.

If the protective power of the breastplate of righteousness was based on my obedience, I was protected on good days and unprotected on bad days. God's Word tells us we can never achieve perfect righteousness by human works, so we'll always have holes in our breastplate—as long as it is based on our performance. So if I fail, tell a lie, or slip up when trying to break deep-seated habits or addictions, am I left defenseless, isolated, and too condemned to pray? Perfect obedience to Christ's commands is what an armored life is designed to produce, but it takes more than knowing the "rules" (the law) to achieve it.

The righteousness which is by faith in Christ

As humans struggling to do right yet subject to mistakes, we need a breastplate that protects our heart at *all* times. We don't deserve it, but we crave a Father who loves us in the midst of our messes. We need a righteousness that does not depend on our efforts but on the perfect performance of another. And that's what Christianity is all about. Paul put his life on the line daily to preach a second kind of righteousness, which comes only by faith in Jesus Christ.[11]

So if we have a weak moment, are spiritually ambushed, are caught in a crossfire of attacks, crack under pressure, and do or say something we regret, we are continually protected by the breastplate of this new kind of righteousness, which is based on faith in what Jesus did for us.

The armor of God is the armor of a renewed mind!

Obeying God, of course, is the easiest way to live in the long run and gives the devil no footholds. So while we never minimize the practical value of personal obedience, neither should we ignore the protective role of God's grace. As a result, we see two layers of righteousness in the breastplate. The righteousness *imputed* by faith in Christ helps produce the righteousness of deeds *imparted* by the Holy Spirit.

Grace for bad days?

Christ's free gift of righteousness assures us of right standing with God at all times. This means that on bad days our prayers are heard, and we can ask for the Holy Spirit's help in the midst of failure. This quality of grace is hard to comprehend in a performance-based world, where the best student gets the A and the hardest worker gets the promotion. But God gave the free gift of righteousness to the imperfect, to sinners, to the weak, and to the wounded living in rebellion. He keeps loving us when we fail, even if *we* have a hard time forgiving our mistakes.

Putting on the breastplate of righteousness means believing God will hear and answer your prayers because of your faith in Christ, even when you have messed up! That's when you really need His encouragement and help. Because if you feel alone, condemned, and that God does not want anything to do with you, you will probably do something to make matters worse.

---

[11] Romans 3:21–22

The experience of God's grace—because it is so unmerited and undeserved—attracts us to the Lord and makes us thank and love Him. Realizing God is in our corner and does not condemn us, even though we are not perfect, takes the pressure off and allows us to breathe. He grants us clarity of mind and helps us rethink and prioritize our lives.

God loves us first of all for who we are, not for what we do. We need to internalize this at such a deep level that we believe Romans 8:1: "There is therefore now *no condemnation* to those who are in Christ Jesus." Overcoming hard-to-break habits and firmly-entrenched thought patterns involves frequent failure, frustration, and condemnation. If you can remember that God loves you in the midst of your shortcomings, that He is pleased you are fighting the enemy even if you don't win every battle, you become stronger.

But if you let condemnation make you feel unworthy of God's help, you will quit praying, give up, and get weaker. God loves and accepts you because of your faith in Jesus Christ, even when your performance is a 3 instead of a 10. Can we abuse or take advantage of God's grace? Sure, whenever we cruise through life and make no effort to obey His Word or become a better person.

Is God soft on sin?

Is God tolerant of our bad behavior? Absolutely not! No matter how much He loves us, His law of sowing and reaping produces bad consequences for every sin. His goal is to help us stop sinning because sin destroys *us*. Sin does not hurt God directly; what hurts God is seeing what sin does to us, our relationships, lives, health, careers, and our children. Sin keeps us from fulfilling our divine purpose, and the Lord wants to free us so we can become all He made us to be.

Having on the breastplate of righteousness means the cannon blasts of condemnation and guilt sent by the enemy don't destroy our confidence or damage our prayer line to God. Christ's righteousness still covers us when our own righteousness is (temporarily) in shambles. When I'm assured of right standing by faith, it's easier to come back to God, make right decisions, and give the enemy no further ground.

The gift of righteousness produces freedom. I'm freer to make right decisions when I know I'm loved and accepted for who I am, when the fear of God's condemnation and judgment has been removed, and I am certain of His ongoing grace.[12]

Our sin is not more powerful than God's love. Before we were Christians, sin separated us from God. Now that we are reconciled to the Father, sin no longer has that power.[13] Did you catch that? Isaiah 59:21 tells us that our sins have separated us from God, but that was before the cross. Jesus came to reconcile imperfect people to the Father. If you think your sin is more powerful than Christ's blood, think again.

Human parents love their children even when they make bad choices, and God is no different. Jesus promised, "And surely I am with you always, to the very end of the age."[14] Always covers a lot of time, every bit of it. If we sin, we sin in His presence because we take Christ into whatever we do.[15] And in the midst of our mess, He is there too, and we have access to His help. Should we be in the mess? No. Will there be consequences to the mess? Yes. But in Him, we find grace, strength, and help, and not condemnation.

What we sow, we reap. What we dirty up, we clean up. But what a blessing to have a Friend who sticks closer than a brother, invisibly there, who sees the good in us, desires to free us, and is always ready to extend a hand up and out of the pit we dug for ourselves. How incredible is the love of God and His amazing grace!

Two sides to righteousness

Paul spoke of two aspects of the breastplate in First Thessalonians.

> But let us who are of the day be sober, putting on *the breastplate of faith and love,* and as a helmet the hope of salvation.
> —*1 Thessalonians 5:8 (italics added)*

The first is that imputed to us by *faith* in Jesus Christ. The second involves the righteousness imparted to us by the Holy Spirit, which means *walking in love* toward our neighbor and doing him no harm. Love and righteousness are connected in the following passage.

---

[12] 1 John 4:18

[13] Sin disrupts our *fellowship* with God until we repent and confess it.

[14] Matthew 28:20 (NIV)

[15] 1 Corinthians 6:15

Owe no one anything except to love one another, for he who loves another has fulfilled the law. For the commandments, "You shall not commit adultery," "You shall not murder," "You shall not steal," "You shall not bear false witness," "You shall not covet," and if there is any other commandment, are all summed up in this saying, namely, "You shall love your neighbor as yourself."

—Romans 13:8–9

The breastplate is laminated with two layers. The inner ply, closest to the heart, is the *righteousness of faith,* giving us access to the grace of God. The outer layer is the *practice of righteousness* that comes from obeying the Word. When our works are imperfect, and sometimes they will be, the outer layer of the breastplate is penetrated, but the inner layer of grace protects our heart. Because of it, we can be confident to seek God's help, repent, make right decisions, and not do something worse out of a hopeless sense of condemnation.

The Shoes of Readiness

When I am fully convinced that God abides with me in the ups and downs of life, not only when I act perfectly, I have successfully put on the breastplate. My soul sighs in relief and rests in Christ. Jesus said, "Come to Me, all you who labor and are heavy laden, and I will give you rest."[16] Paul said in Romans 5:1, "Therefore, having been justified [made righteous] by faith, we have *peace with God* through our Lord Jesus Christ." Peace comes when we put on the breastplate. The psalmist said, "Righteousness and peace have kissed."[17]

In that rest of conscience, I enjoy peace with God and experience His love. I am accepted just as I am, adopted into His family as a son or daughter with full rights and privileges. I am everlastingly grateful for His grace, and my heart overflows with thanksgiving, for God has captured my love by His undeserved favor, by loving and accepting one so unworthy. The vine of my gratitude grows upward until it wraps itself around God's heart, blooming profusely in the sunshine of His countenance. A desire rises within me to repay Him who loves me more than

---

[16] Matthew 11:28

[17] Psalm 85:10

any other. I become willing to submit to and follow Him, so I can stay close to my soul's companion, everlasting help, and choicest friend.

In that heartfelt response to the grace of the breastplate, I have strapped on shoes of *readiness* (or *preparation)*. The Amplified Bible expresses the sense of the original Greek.

> And having shod your feet in preparation [to face the enemy with the firm-footed stability, the promptness, and *the readiness produced by the good news*] of the Gospel of peace.
> —*Ephesians 6:15 (AMP, italics added)*

When read carefully, the Bible does not say our feet are shod with peace but with the *readiness (or preparation) produced by the peace* that comes from the righteousness of faith. Shoes of readiness are worn by those whose hearts rest in grace. They are shoes of thankfulness, shoes of yieldedness, shoes of service, shoes of submission to the will of God.

Shoes and feet, of course, symbolize our spiritual walk. When we strap on the battle sandals of readiness, we are yielded and ready to go wherever our Commander in Chief sends us. Putting on the sandals means surrendering our will to the Lord's will and allowing Him to direct our paths. Those with their battle sandals on say with Jesus, "...nevertheless, not what I will, but what You will."[18]

When we go where He sends us, we have secure footing because the sandals of God's will are securely strapped on, have cleats like a Roman soldier's sandals, and won't slip. We are *ready* to stand immovable as conflict swirls around us. Of course, if we revert back to doing our own will, the sandals slide off, and our bare feet are pierced by every sharp thing in our self-willed path. Are you prepared, ready, and yielded to do what the Lord would have you do? If so, you have your battle sandals on!

As one prepared to serve the Lord, you have a message: In Christ the power of the oppressor is broken, good things are coming, and our God reigns! When we faithfully deliver the good news, the Bible says we have beautiful feet.[19]

---

[18] Mark 14:36

[19] Isaiah 52:7, Romans 10:15

The Shield of Faith

Now that we are yielded to our Commander's will and have entered the battlefield, we encounter opposition in the form of "flaming arrows,"[20] troubling thoughts of doubt, discouragement, depression, fear, and unworthiness. At this point, we must take up the shield of faith or the warfare in our mind will stop us from going forward. Lifting up the shield means holding God's promises between us and the flaming arrows to quench their fire. Volume 2 of this series, *Tearing Down Strongholds,* will show you how to do this effectively.

The Helmet of Salvation

Like modern soldiers, Roman soldiers wore helmets to protect their heads from injury during battle. We need a helmet to protect our minds in spiritual warfare. But wait a minute! Every piece of armor we've described so far protects our minds. The truth of God's Word defends us from lies and deception. The breastplate protects us from feelings of unworthiness, lack of acceptance by God, guilt, and shame. Putting on the shoes means laying down our will to walk in God's paths. The shield of faith extinguishes the troubling thoughts launched into our minds. *So what more can the helmet do that hasn't already been done?*

Paul gives us a clue in First Thessalonians where he calls the helmet, "the *hope* of salvation."[21] Hope in modern English is a weak word. When we say, "I hope so," we often mean, "I wish it were so, but I'm not sure it will work out." But hope in the original Greek meant a *confident expectation* with an *optimistic outlook.* Christian hope says, "With God on my side, all this trouble will work to my advantage." The world lives in cynicism, skepticism, pessimism, discouragement, and despair. They say, "What's the use?" "Why try?" "Just give up." "Have another drink."

But Christians who strap on their helmets have a *positive attitude of hope, a confident expectation of victory.* They are cheerful in the midst of trouble and with God's help expect to win every battle. Why? They have full trust in the power, faithfulness, and reliability of God. Paul pointed

---

[20] Ephesians 6:16, "fiery darts" in some older versions
[21] 1 Thessalonians 5:8

out Abraham's amazing posture of hope, "who, contrary to hope, in hope believed, so that he became the father of many nations..."[22] Even when it looked impossible, Abraham believed God.

You can have on the best armor in the world, but if you don't have hope that inspires your will to fight, you are defeated before the battle starts. Putting on the helmet means adjusting your life's attitude from being negative, wounded, and pessimistic, to being strong, conquering, and victorious in Christ. Nobody goes to war hoping to lose. They go to war because there is something to win, something to gain, some spoils to gather. You put on the armor of God to win something! What are some "spoils" of winning in Christian conflict? *Personal freedom from the enemy! Salvation of souls! Being a blessing to all nations (starting in your neighborhood)!*

We learn from experience that the Lord brings us through every difficulty and trial.[23] So, as we grow in Christ, our attitude should change from hoping for a little victory once in a while to expecting victory all the time. Paul wrote that God *"always leads us in triumph in Christ."*[24] Wouldn't you agree that "always" is a strong but inspired word? Paul should know—he went through more trouble than anyone I know.[25] John wrote, *"And this is the victory that has overcome the world—our faith."*[26] Both Paul and John wore the helmet, the confident expectation that salvation would work everything to their advantage for the benefit of the kingdom of God.

The winning attitude

In our culture the closest thing to the helmet of salvation is the attitude of soldiers and professional athletes who prepare to overcome adversity and win every battle and game. They never give up. I love fourth quarter, come-from-behind victories. What a thrill when my team rallies, scores, and seizes the day. A basketball team may trail the whole game, but a buzzer-beating three-pointer changes a loss into a win. It's never

---

[22] Romans 4:18
[23] Romans 5:3–5
[24] 2 Corinthians 2:14
[25] 2 Corinthians 11:23–33
[26] 1 John 5:4

over till it's over. You may think you're losing, but a champion lives in your heart—Jesus! He never gives up and doesn't want you to let go of your dream. You can do it. You will make it. You are an overcomer!

In our culture the closest thing to the helmet of salvation is the attitude of soldiers and professional athletes, who prepare to overcome adversity and win every battle and game.

Professional athletes think like warriors. A sports reporter once asked winning Stanford football coach David Shaw about his team's prospects against a higher-ranked team. He answered something like this: *It's not who we play that we focus on. It's how we play.* He gave intimidation no place by focusing on his team's strengths. Our God is a big God, and the weapons He has given us are more powerful than the enemy's.

Professional athletes must live in the present, not the past. A quarterback who throws two interceptions in the third quarter can still win if he shakes off the mistakes, doesn't get rattled, and keeps his head in the game. But if he gets tied up with self-condemnation, he'll become ineffective. Putting on the helmet of salvation means forgetting the past, focusing on the present, and preparing for the future. Paul voted to kill and imprison Christians in his past, but he learned not to let the enemy keep bringing their faces before his mind. He kept his eyes on the finish line and the prize.[27]

We are to put on the helmet of *salvation.* The essence of the word is "being made safe." Christians often narrow the meaning to having an eternal home in heaven, but Jesus wants to "save" us in *temporal* things as well. In the Bible, the words *save* and *salvation* also speak of healing, physical safety, and deliverance from calamities, demons, storms, and prison.

In all things, then, both eternal and temporal, Christians are to strap on a confident expectation and a winning attitude. Through faith in Christ we have a home in heaven, but while we are on earth our Savior

---

[27] Philippians 3:13–14

heals, delivers, and provides for us in earthly, temporal difficulties, too. Sometimes people think God does not care about the temporal things of earth, yet He was the one who made every material thing and declared it very good. He is touched with the feelings of our (temporal) infirmities. Yes, the eternal is all that ultimately matters, but God loves us enough to care and provide for us while we live here on earth.

Here are three easy steps to keeping a positive, confident outlook:

- *Don't be alarmed or surprised by resistance.*[28]
- *Encourage yourself in the Lord*[29] by remembering how God helped you in the past.
- *Prepare for victory* by confessing your faith.[30]

Putting on the helmet, the confident expectation of salvation, defends us from the discouragement and depression so common in the world. When we have on the helmet, we see the glass half full (not half empty) and won't quit or throw in the towel. Because our hope is in the Lord, we remain upbeat, confident, and willing to move forward in battle.

The Sword of the Spirit

Paul also told us to take "the sword of the Spirit, which is the Word of God." The truth of God's Word has contributed to every piece of armor, but a change is made now from defense to offense. While a sword may be used defensively to parry an opponent's thrust, it is primarily an *offensive* weapon. As the army of the Lord, our posture is not merely defensive, but we are expected to attack and take new ground in confidence of victory.

It's interesting that the phrase, "the sword of the Spirit, which is the *Word* of God," does not use the common word for written Scripture, *graphe*. If you own a Bible, you have *graphe,* but *graphe* is not the sword. However, when you open the *graphe,* and the Holy Spirit breathes into you understanding about a verse, the *graphe* becomes a living *logos*. The sword is not the *logos,* but it definitely comes from the *logos*. The sword of the Spirit is the *rhema—a spoken, uttered,* or *declared Word.* It's not

---

[28] John 16:33
[29] 1 Samuel 30:6–8
[30] 1 Samuel 17:26, 36–37, 45–46

the whole Bible, but the verse the Holy Spirit made alive that is relevant to our situation.[31]

Understanding the Word is not enough. Only when we utter it aloud can it deliver lethal blows, like the Roman soldier's short sword in personal combat. The spoken word releases God's power into the atmosphere around us.

Imagine that each verse of Scripture is an atom. The tremendous energy stored in the nucleus of an atom can be released when the atom is split. Likewise, great energy is encapsulated in each verse of the Bible, and the Holy Spirit releases that energy when He fills our hearts to overflowing with a fresh understanding of it. If we then vocalize that verse as a *rhema* Word, we unleash a wave of divine energy into the spiritual realm. This amazing power removes mountains and tears down strongholds.

The devil cannot withstand the uttered Word of God, for it is the same Word that judges him. He has no armor to resist it. The Lord will consume the lawless one with the "breath of His mouth," His spoken Word.[32] When Jesus returns on His white horse, a two-edged sword will come forth from His mouth—the uttered *rhema* Word of God.

Jesus demonstrated how to use the sword of the Spirit when He was tempted. Three times He declared to the devil, "It is written,"[33] and then quoted a single verse. The devil was forced to back off. So much power resides in the spoken Word of God that it was Jesus' weapon of choice. Since we are made in His image, the same sword works for us. The *rhema* Word gives us authority over opposing strongholds.

I know what it means to have my heart filled with understanding as the Holy Spirit turns the *graphe* into the *logos*. But using the sword of the Spirit requires me to declare it. Out of the abundance of the heart the mouth must speak. We release the burning *logos* in our hearts with a fiery proclamation, an authoritative *rhema* command inspired by the Holy Spirit. If you've never spoken the Word of God into the invisible

---

[31] Tony Evans, *Victory in Spiritual Warfare*, (Eugene, OR: Harvest House Publishers, 2011), pp. 121–132. Also check out Pastor Tony Evan's video series and workbook, *Victory in Spiritual Warfare*, available from Lifeway.com.

[32] 2 Thessalonians 1:8, Revelation 19:15

[33] Matthew 4:4, 7, 10

realm like a commander with great authority, you have not yet taken up the sword of the Spirit.

This uttered word is an offensive force. *Rhema* words not only send away demons, but God's Word speaks new vision into our lives. When Paul received the Macedonian call from the Spirit of God, "Come over to Macedonia and help us," his missionary party took the gospel of Christ to Europe for the first time.[34] This *rhema* word of guidance was a trumpet call for Paul to go on offense and take new ground in faith. It moved him to a new continent and a new dimension of service.

> ### *Understanding the Word is not enough. Only when we utter it aloud can it deliver lethal blows, like the Roman soldier's short sword in personal combat.*

Rhema-guided leaders direct organizations into victory, new territory, and the recapturing of lost ground for Jesus. Their inspired words speak fresh vision and direction, moving the kingdom of God forward in faith. God may call you to go forward with an express word or He may make something in Scripture so real that it becomes a divine call. He emboldens you to speak the dream and live it out. His inspired words slash the chains of inertia that hold you back, as you go on the offense to claim new territory for the glory of God. If you face resistance, take out the sword and speak the *rhema* word that God gave you.

The Lance of Prayer

In his excellent book on the armor of God, *Dressed to Kill*, Rick Renner describes how every Roman soldier carried one final weapon.[35] The lance or spear was an essential part of the soldier's full equipment, and he did not go to battle without it. Lances came in many lengths, weights, shapes, and materials. Some were for throwing, some were for hand-to-hand combat, and some were made completely of iron.

---

[34] Acts 16:9–10

[35] Rick Renner, *Dressed to Kill*, 4th ed. (Tulsa, OK: Teach All Nations, 1991, 2007), pp. 435–463.

Paul did not mention the lance specifically, but he told us to put on the *whole armor* of God, including *every* piece of armor and weaponry. Just as the Roman soldier had *all kinds* of lances and spears to use, Paul exhorted us in Ephesians 6:18 to pray with *all kinds* of prayer and supplication in the Spirit. Prayer is a lance that can be thrown or thrust from a distance. The sword is for hand-to-hand combat.

Like the lance, prayer is a powerful weapon, and different kinds of prayer can be used according to the need. Prayer has a longer reach than the Roman lance since it can be directed anywhere in the world. When we use the long lance of prayer *before* engaging the enemy, we don't face so much hand-to-hand combat.

Here are three of the most powerful kinds of prayer:

- *The prayer of authority*, or *commanding prayer*, is based on the victory Jesus Christ won on the cross. This prayer is prayed in the authority of Jesus' name. In Mark 11:22–24, Jesus prophesied that we would speak to mountains (hindrances, obstacles, and spiritual forces) and command them to be cast into the sea.

- *Preemptive prayer* attacks and thwarts problems before they occur. It nips trouble in the bud. We talked about this in an earlier chapter, so pray *before* you go into every situation, and things will turn out much better.

- *Praying in the Spirit*: Praying always with all kinds of prayer and supplication *in the Spirit* includes praying with other tongues, or Holy Spirit-assisted praying. The Holy Spirit resides in your spirit, so release Him to pray in, with, and through your spirit according to the will of God.[36] There is a difference between praying with your spirit and praying with your mind.[37] Praying in the Spirit includes praying in "warfare tongues," an emphatic and effective kind of prayer. We are also to pray with our minds.

---

[36] Romans 8:26-27
[37] 1 Corinthians 14:14-15

Spiritual warfare requires *all kinds* of prayer and supplication before and during the battle.

Putting on the armor of light is renewing the mind

Putting on the whole armor of God involves progressive revelations. It means *renewing our minds* in these seven key areas. Thinking like Jesus transforms, arms, and protects us. The revelations of truth, righteousness, readiness, and hope of salvation, represented by the girdle, breastplate, shoes, and helmet, become embedded in our spirits. They become part of who we are. The shield, the sword, and the lance we take up daily as required.

What kind of challenges do you face?

- Are you confused by *the lies and deception* that abound in the culture? Wrap the belt of truth about your life, and let the Word of God settle every question.

- Is a personal sense of *unworthiness* or *guilt over sin* separating you from God? Put your trust in the breastplate of righteousness. Jesus obtained right standing for you on the cross. Relax and believe the good news. Your right standing with God is not based on your works but on what Jesus did for you on the cross.

- If you are *not yielded to the will of God* and ready to serve Him, then you haven't fully received what Jesus has done for you. You are forgiven, made new, and made righteous in the eyes of God. Let go and let God fill your heart with peace. Out of that peace you will find a readiness to walk in the paths of God and desire the Lord's will for your life more than your own. Pray like Jesus, "Not my will, but Yours, be done."[38]

- Are you experiencing *troubling thoughts,* those constant *doubts, fears,* and *what-if's*? Take up the shield of faith. You can trust God's Word of promise. Hold the promises like a shield between you and the thoughts or circumstances.

---

[38] Luke 22:42

- Maybe you are discouraged and a *lack of hope* keeps you from moving forward. The helmet, the hope of salvation, is the warrior's attitude of confident expectation. Expect to win every battle because God always causes you to triumph in Christ. All things will work to your advantage and the kingdom's.

- Are you under attack and *not sure how to fight back?* Take the sword of the Spirit and speak the Word of God with authority. Like Jesus, declare "It is written!" and then quote the verse the Holy Spirit gives you.

- See *a problem coming* and want to thwart it before it happens? Use the lance of prayer and spiritually strike the opposition before you go into hand-to-hand combat, asking for God's protection, wisdom, and guidance.

The armor of God helps us stand against the wiles of the devil in every battle. Our posture of faith, of leaning on and trusting God's Word, draws the protective envelope of the whole armor of God around us.

> *Father, I gird my loins about with truth, embracing the wisdom of Your Word and its ability to guide my life. I put on the breastplate of righteousness by faith in Jesus. I am in right standing with You on good days and bad days, and You hear my prayers for help. I lace up the sandals of readiness produced by the peace of being right with you. I am Your servant, submitted to Your will for my life, allowing you to direct my steps. I take the shield of faith in Your promises, with which I can quench all the flaming thought arrows the wicked one puts in my mind. I put on the helmet, the confident hope and expectation of salvation (including deliverance and healing in this world and eternal life in the world to come). I take the sword of the Spirit and speak the authoritative Word of God. I pray always with the long reach of prayer and supplication in the Spirit. I thank You that You are my shield, my exceedingly great reward. In Jesus' name, I pray. Amen.*

SECRET #19: Put on the full "armor of light." As you receive the revelation of each piece, you are protected from the lies, deceptions, discouragement, and flaming arrows of the enemy. Be encouraged! You are an overcomer because the Spirit of Jesus Christ, the Champion, lives in you.

What to Do When Attacked

Turn: Turn your heart to the light of Christ.

Belt: Wrap the truth of God's Word around your life.

Breastplate: Believe the free gift of righteousness by faith.

Shoes: Yield to God's will (walk) for your life.

Shield: Replace doubt with faith in God's promises.

Helmet: Confidently expect salvation (temporal and eternal).

Sword: Declare the Word aloud.

Lance: Pierce the darkness with every kind of prayer.

Closing Prayer

Father, in the name of Jesus and by the power of the Holy Spirit, grant that each person who reads this book may receive a blessing appropriate to their life and circumstances; that their relationship to You may be strengthened as their understanding grows and abounds; and that they may walk in the love of Jesus Christ to all. Amen.

Index of Prayers

R

S

T

About Michael Christian

Shortly after graduating from college, Michael Christian experienced a work-related accident in which he narrowly escaped death and suffered a serious concussion. In order to heal and restore his mind, Mike was inspired to hand copy Bible verses for four hours a day. In doing this, he quickly received healing for his brain. But rather than stopping, he continued on copying Scripture to renew his mind in the knowledge of God. This began his love for the Bible, which reveals itself in his passion for the Word of God and depth of insight as a Bible teacher. Michael met and married his wife Debbie at Jubilee Church in Paradise, California, where he served for twenty-five years as an Associate Pastor. The Christians have two married sons, two wonderful daughters-in-law, and two grandsons. Pastor Mike's interests range from Bible teaching to computers, graphic design, audio and video production, and construction. His hobbies include photography and gardening.

A Free Gift from Michael and a Study Guide

G reat job on finishing *The Armor of Light!* I hope it has helped you increase the level of victory in your life. You can download a free Thank You gift at:

https://michaelchristian.us/armor-of-light-resources/gift

If the book has been a blessing, would you post a positive review on *The Armor of Light* page on Amazon.com? A few words sharing how the book helped you will encourage others to read it.

Downloadable Study Guide

The Armor of Light is perfect for Bible study groups, and you can download a 44-page Study Guide at:

https://michaelchristian.us/armor-of-light-resources/

Please don't overlook the volume discount pricing available on the website. Buying in bulk makes the book more affordable for groups.

https://michaelchristian.us/product/armor-book/

THE VICTORIOUS LIVING SERIES

VOLUMES 2 AND 3 ARE COMING SOON!

Volume 2

TEARING DOWN STRONGHOLDS

How to Fight the Good Fight of Faith

Tearing Down Strongholds identifies life's most common battlegrounds—the mind, the flesh, personal relationships, and fighting the good fight of faith. It teaches you how to extinguish the flaming thought arrows the enemy shoots into your mind. If left to burn, these will build strongholds in your mind, will, and emotions that will hold you in bondage for years. You need strategies for tearing down these strongholds, overcoming your flesh, protecting your relationships, and keeping the Word of God between you and your problems. The book includes original illustrations, prayers, and a life secret at the end of each chapter.

Volume 3

DECLARATIONS OF TRUTH

How to Pray God's Word with Authority

The perfect companion to Volumes 1 and 2, *Declarations of Truth* provides inspired prayers and Scripture-based affirmations to help you demolish personal strongholds in over fifty areas of life. Breakthrough comes as you wield the sword of the Spirit—the uttered Word of God. As you declare Scripture aloud, you create seismic shifts in your spiritual atmosphere.

These books will help you fulfill your divine purpose
and finish your race with joy.

Made in United States
Orlando, FL
02 February 2023

29393841R00102